NATIONAL PRAISE FOR DEREK FOSTER

"His (Derek Foster's) seductively simple approach...
resonated with tens of thousands of Canadians who
bought his bestselling books..."   — *Globe and Mail*

"Thanks to a healthy stock portfolio, Derek Foster
retired when he was 34 years old."   — *Toronto Star*

"Thanks to a solid investment plan and a knack for
picking the right stocks he (Derek Foster) was able to
retire, mortgage-free, at the age of 34."
                              — *ROBTV (forerunner to BNN)*

"He's (Derek Foster) playing his very own game, which
he's winning..."   — *National Post*

"...– and he did it by turning the whole concept of
what it means to save for retirement on its head."
                              — *Moneysense Magazine*

"While Warren Buffett is known as the Oracle of Omaha,
investment whiz Derek Foster could be labelled the
Wise Man of Wasaga Beach."   — *Toronto Sun*

STOP WORKING TOO
You Still Can!

Library and Archives Canada Cataloguing in Publication
Foster, Derek, 1970–
　　Stop working too, you still can! : safe beginner strategies from Canada's millionaire investor / Derek Foster.
ISBN 978-0-9736960-3-5
1. Retirement income–Planning. 2. Investments. 3. Finance, Personal.
I. Title.
HG179.F6693 2009　　332.024'014　　C2009-906008-6

Published by
Foster, Underhill Financial Press
Suite 508, 900 Greenbank Road
Ottawa, ON Canada K2J 4P6

Phone toll free at: 1 888 686 STOP (1 888 686 7867)
or 613 823 2143
www.stopworking.ca

Design/formatting/production: WeMakeBooks.ca
Printed and bound in Canada

STOP WORKING TOO

You Still Can!

Safe Beginner Strategies from
Canada's
Millionaire Investor

FOSTER, UNDERHILL FINANCIAL PRESS

LEGAL DISCLAIMER

This book is intended to show you a strategy that you might want to consider for investing.

However, you must realize that I am not a professional with regard to any of the information I've provided in this book. I am merely presenting a strategy that I feel might be of interest to you. I am not an expert in economic, legal, taxation, investing, realty, or any other financial or related matters. The examples I provide are just that – examples. These are intended for illustrative purposes only. They are not an indication of what rate of return or future amount of money you might have if you followed the specific examples. They are only presented to illustrate the general concepts. Before initiating any of the strategies outlined, seek the advice of a competent professional to help you.

The book is intended as a general guide and should not be viewed as the ultimate source for financial information. Further research is needed and assistance must be sought from a qualified expert, before any action is taken by the reader. For further information, there are many sources of information listed in this book. The information offered there might be incomplete, inaccurate, or out of date, so the reader should verify any of this information before acting on it.

For full disclosure, I must say that I (Derek Foster) owned many of the securities mentioned in this book. The reader must also understand that any investing activity entails certain degrees of risk. Although certain securities are presented in the book, the reader must understand that these securities do carry risk and should seek the advice from a qualified expert before acting upon any of the information.

Furthermore, this book might contain various errors, omissions, or mistakes of either a typographical nature or within the content itself. The reader must not rely on the accuracy of any of the information given, but should seek proper verification.

The author (Derek Foster) and the publisher (Foster Underhill Financial Press) shall have neither liability nor responsibility to any person or other legal entity with respect to any sort of loss or damage or perceived damage caused, or alleged to have been caused by the information provided in this book. By reading this, you fully accept these conditions. If for any reason, you do not wish to be bound by any or all of the above conditions, you many simply return this book to the publisher for a full refund.

ACKNOWLEDGEMENTS

There are many people I need to thank – without their help this book would not have been possible.

Once again, I need to thank my wife Hyeeun. Your support and understanding were instrumental in me completing this work. Thanks again for "holding down the fort."

Special thanks to my mom Tina Colonnese whose critical thinking skills, valuable input and viewpoints from a senior's perspective allowed me to expand upon my existing ideas. I enjoyed "burning the midnight oil" with you mom.

To Todd Lavigne, thanks for offering your "brutal" honesty in assessing my writing – which helped me to keep the proper focus. Your insights were helpful and often pragmatic.

To George von Jagow, I cannot thank you enough for helping me understand the subtleties involved in RRSP mortgages – your extensive knowledge in this area helped me greatly. I appreciate you taking time from your busy schedule to offer your insights.

To Stephane Lachapelle, thank you for offering your feedback and thoughts on important sections of the book. Your input was appreciated.

Finally, to James Hymas, who offered additional information on preferred shares – thank you.

TABLE OF CONTENTS...

RULES OF INVESTING:
Rule #1: Don't lose money.
Rule #2: Remember rule #1.
— *Warren Buffett*

1

WANT TO STOP WORKING?...
YOU MAY BE CLOSER
THAN YOU THINK

"The art is not in making money,
but in keeping it."
– Proverb

This book is a simple guide offering various strategies
that will help you stop working while avoiding undue
risk – without the complex financial jargon. If you think
you will never stop working because you have lost money
due to the recent financial turmoil or don't feel you've
saved enough – then this book is for YOU. If you get
concerned when you see your portfolio decline by 50%
or more in a matter of a few months, then this book is

for YOU. I will show you how you might already have more income than you thought. You'll learn some simple, little-known strategies that will help you *lower your risk while still being able to retire.*

This book is NOT about making you a millionaire – it's about ensuring that when you want to stop working, you will be able to do so and enjoy a comfortable lifestyle. I have written about my thoughts on money and investing in *"STOP WORKING: Here's How You Can!"*, *"The Lazy Investor"*, and *"Money for Nothing"* – so what is the main difference with this book?

In my first book, I wrote about how I was able to leave the rat race at 34. I offered some very effective strategies that had worked very well for me. My second book outlined a simple investment strategy that my kids were employing to build wealth automatically. My third book, which was written for sophisticated investors, offered a different approach I use to invest. The point is that all three books related to what *I* was doing in *my* investment life.

This new book was written entirely for *you*. It looks at realistic factors that may affect *your* situation and offers concrete ideas on how *you* can stop working. It's not a *"this is what I did"* book, but instead a *"this is what you can do"* book. This book builds on my other investing strategies – but ties everything together so you can stop working too!

Contrary to what many people say, having money is important – BUT only to a point. I've always felt that once you reach a certain level of comfort, more money doesn't necessarily add quality to your life. Let me explain this further with an example.

Let's assume you are on a tight budget and can only afford macaroni and cheese for dinner every day – and only small portions. In this situation, having a little more money adds a lot more enjoyment to your life – so earning more money is very important in this situation. However, once you've reached the point where you have lots of food available, enough to cook a few steaks on the barbeque from time and time and dine out on occasion – life is pretty good. Moving from this situation to one where you can dine on caviar daily and wash it down with bottles of Dom Perignon Champagne, although a nice option – won't make a huge difference to your happiness.

This book aims to show you how to keep the "steaks on the barbeque" level of comfort *without you needing to take undue risks.* Remember the old Aesop fable where there was a country mouse and a city mouse? The city mouse had more luxuries but also lived constantly in fear while the country mouse lived a relatively comfortable life without any worries. This book is for the "country mice" out there – people who are not interested in taking huge gambles while striving for a comfortable lifestyle. If you would rather gamble your "steaks on the barbeque" for a chance at "caviar and Dom Perignon" – with the risk of being left with just "macaroni and cheese", then this book is of no benefit to you.

Few investors are aware of these low-risk, little-known strategies, because if they were the financial industry (ie banks, brokers, money managers) would earn less money. If you feel guilty knowing that by following these ideas you might end up with more money in your pocket, but the banks would earn less profit – then don't read this.

I've written this book in response to countless emails I've received (especially during the recent stock market turmoil). Knowledge is the key to removing your anxiety about your financial future and getting you on your way – so you can stop working and stop worrying.

2

THE ADVANTAGE OF "KNOWING THE SYSTEM"

"There is no shame in not knowing; the shame lies in not finding out."

– Russian Proverb

After graduating from university I decided to pursue a backpacking adventure across Europe. The amazing sites, interesting people, and delicious food were wonderful experiences. The most delicious food I tasted was in Italy – but my experience there drove home the idea that things are not always what they seem.

I had met a few other people from Canada and we had decided to travel together for a while. So off we went – exploring the world...when we spotted a restaurant. The wonderful smell of food filled the air and we took a quick look at the menu on display. Since we were all on a tight budget, prices were important, but a quick glance at the menu showed pretty reasonable prices. So we decided to eat there.

At the end of our meal we were presented a bill that was more than double the price we expected. Our meal prices were listed, but in addition to these we saw a charge for sitting down, an additional charge for bread, another cost for water, and a built-in added gratuity. We did not know whether or not these charges were customary, so we paid our bill and left. Our budget for that day had been blown by these extra charges.

Over time we learned what charges to expect and how to avoid them in many cases.

The point in sharing this scenario with you is when you find yourself in unfamiliar surroundings, the uncertainty of not knowing what should be charged causes anxiety. A similar situation can occur when you bring your car in for repairs and you're not sure if the mechanic is overcharging you. Another example might be when you take a ride in a taxi in an unfamiliar city. You might have experienced a driver who drove much more than necessary to get you to your destination so that he could increase your final fare.

So how about your investments? Are you paying more than you should? Can you make a few minor adjustments and reduce the amount of financial fees you're forced to pay? Are there some low-risk investments that offer solid returns that you have never been shown? Are there tax strategies you can use in order to reduce the amount you pay in taxes? In many cases, small changes (that are virtually unknown to most people outside the system) can yield enormous results! That's the first secret – you must know how the system works. Many people would rather work a lot of overtime in order to earn more money rather than arrange their finances such that they can make more money without any extra work. The only reason this is the case is because they don't know the system. I will outline simple, comprehensive strategies in a common sense format without using the complex financial jargon found in most financial and investing information.

The aim of this book is to show you some of the financial industry secrets (that they might not want you to know) so that you can use this information to earn more money and reach your goal of retirement more quickly. A quick example that most people face at some point in their lives will help illustrate the power of this idea.

Did you know many people think the "posted rate" at banks is the rate they have to pay for a mortgage? In most cases, this rate is negotiable – just like the price of a car is. Even many "set price" car dealers have room to negotiate even though they want you to believe they don't. The reality is that businesses would like to maximize profits so they won't give you the best deal right away. However, if you spend a few minutes explaining your personal situation and suggest you might want to shop around, the mortgage loan officer might offer you a better deal. Banks will often reduce their posted rates by half a percent or more if asked.

"What's the big deal about half a percent?", you might ask. Let's take a quick look at effect of this seemingly small amount.

If you get a $200,000 mortgage for 25 years at 5%, your monthly cost would be around $1,163. If you are able to reduce that rate to 4.5% with five minutes of discussion because you know that banks usually don't expect to receive the posted rate, your monthly payment instantly drops to $1,107. So many people look at that and think – big deal. Your savings are only ($1,163 – $1,107=) $56. But the key is that for 5 minutes of your time, you could save $56 per month *for 25 years*. The net result is almost *$17,000 in savings* over the life of the mortgage! In other words, by asking for a reduced rate, you earn enough to buy a new car – FREE! I'd rather ask for a simple rate reduction than work countless hours of overtime. How about you?

The main point I'm trying to make is that you should have at least a little scepticism when dealing with financial matters – the same sort of thinking you have when you buy a car. When you walk into the dealership, you will listen to the salesperson, but you won't blindly believe everything they tell you. Their role is to get the highest possible profit for the vehicle they are selling you. From your perspective, you are there to buy a vehicle at the best possible price.

It's the same when dealing with your investments. You should always be asking yourself, "Are my goals and those of this company perfectly aligned?" If the goals are not aligned you need to find out how the company earns its profits – so you can understand what motivates them.

For example, let's take this book you are holding in your hand. What was my motivation for writing it? First off – I really enjoy writing books – it's very rewarding to be able to share my knowledge and experiences and help you follow your goals to retire in comfort. Second, writing books is very rewarding for me from a financial perspective – I earn money from selling my books.

The more people who buy this book, the more money I make – it's that simple. The price of this book is in line with other financial books, so there's no real negotiation between you and I with regards to price. As for the information, I hope to offer simple, personal and valuable information that helps you reach your goal of a comfortable retirement. If I am able to accomplish that, you'll probably tell others about my book – which may ultimately create more sales for me. If the information is not useful, you won't buy the book (or recommend it to other people), so there's a large incentive for me to make it useful to you. Therefore – our goals are basically aligned. I want to produce a useful book so this creates more sales for me – and you want an informative book that details important financial information that you can use to your advantage.

In the mortgage example earlier in this chapter, the goals are not aligned. The bank wants to earn as much as possible (by charging a higher rate) while you'd like to save money (by getting a cheaper rate). Regardless, the bank still wants your business. By you making the suggestion that you will take your business elsewhere, the bank may be motivated to consider a reduced interest rate. Knowledge is power and possessing this knowledge in combination with making a slight adjustment in your behaviour (asking for a reduced interest rate), allows you to potentially save thousands of dollars (as we saw with the $17,000 savings).

This book will offer some simple ideas or strategies you might not know about and reveal some basic financial secrets that will help you earn more money – just by knowing the rules of the game. These are the secrets the experts will never reveal – because it's not in their best interest. Let's start by looking at the number one, risk–free, high–return activity you can do with your money.

3

FROM DEBTORS PRISONS
TO WAGE SLAVERY

"We don't have a trillion-dollar
debt because we haven't taxed
enough; we have a trillion-dollar
debt because we spend too much"
– Ronald Reagan

If you are already completely debt–free, congratulations! By debt–free I mean that your mortgage is completely paid off. It also means you have no car loans or leases, no credit card debt, and no personal loans to pay of any kind. If this describes your situation, give yourself a big pat on the back because you are in a small minority of the North American population. If you are completely debt-free, then skip ahead to the next chapter.

If not, then you are part of the majority. Read on to learn some tips for getting out of debt. For example, ideas about paying off your mortgage years earlier and saving you thousands of dollars or learning to get the credit card companies to PAY YOU rather than YOU PAYING THEM.

Let's begin with a little history...

Prior to the mid 19th century debtors' prisons were a common way to deal with unpaid debt. During the Middle Ages, debtors, were locked up until their families paid their debt. If the head of the family – the father at that time, was locked up, the whole family was destined for poverty as the main income provider could no longer provide. In fact one of the main reasons we are so familiar with characters such as Ebenezer Scrooge is because Charles Dickens' father was sent to one of these prisons and this public shame had an impact on Dickens for the rest of his life. Although debtors prisons are a thing of the past (in most countries), debt still imprisons many people and is also a major factor in divorce in our society.

If you carry debt, you are forced to work to earn money but a portion of that money "disappears" into the black hole of debt repayment. A large portion of your income gets gobbled up by interest on your debts. If you want to retire with a comfortable lifestyle, the number one risk-free action you can take is to pay off your debt. Using an analogy, let's suppose you plant a "money tree" (representing your investments). The tree is going to provide you with a constant flow of income, but you must nurture it first. You need to water it regularly (water representing the money you need to save and invest to secure your future). Suppose you need to fill up a bucket with water (invest your money) in order to water the tree which is some distance away. If the bucket is filled with holes (representing debt), it will be empty by the time you reach the tree as all the water will drain out – just as debt drains away your income reducing the amount you have left to live on and invest. No matter how much water you add, it ends up completely gone because it leaks through the holes in the bucket before you get to water your "money tree". The end result is that the tree withers and dies and you are left with nothing.

In this situation, the solution is to plug the holes (pay off your debt so it stops draining away your income). As you plug the holes, you are able to get a little water to the tree and it begins to grow a little. Once you have plugged all the holes, you are able to provide enough water for the tree to flourish! It's the same with debt – once it's paid off, life becomes a whole lot easier. Becoming debt-free was the foundation of my plan to quit the worka-day world.

If you do nothing else for yourself financially, pay off your debts (and then stay out of debt)!

Once you pay off your debt you will suddenly feel a sense of freedom. It's empowering! During the recent stock market crash my portfolio suffered a decline along with every other investor but due to the fact that I carry no debt – no mortgage payments, no car lease, no credit card debt and no bank loans – it had a limited impact on my family. I didn't worry about ending up in a card-board box at the side of the street. Since I don't have any debt, my financial needs are much lower than people who carry debt.

So how can you eliminate debt (or plug the "holes" in your watering bucket). The first step is to stop punch-ing new holes into the bucket! In other words, stop adding to your debt. When you see a flashy new gadget you just "have to get", why not save up for it? If the idea of delaying what you want does not appeal to you, why not set aside a certain sum of money every time you get your paycheck (and allow it to build up *without spending it*). That way the next time you see something you want – you have the money to pay for it.

Once you've stopped taking on new debt, the next step is to gradually pay down the debt you've accumulated. One way to can pay debt off more quickly is to find a way to reduce the interest rates you are being charged. For example, you can sometimes consolidate all your debt into one loan payment at a lower interest rate – then focus on paying down that loan as quickly as possible. If this applies to you, make an appointment at your bank and see what options they might have available to help you.

If you are not able to consolidate your debt into one loan, the next best strategy is to eliminate your debts one by one – starting with the debt which charges the highest interest first. This is usually credit cards, so let's start there:

1. Credit Cards

If you go back a couple of generations, people paid for things with cash. If they did not have enough money to afford something, they would save their money until they had accumulated enough to make the purchase. Aside from mortgages, debts were avoided. Then society changed. We began to want things immediately, whether we could afford them or not. We've become a society that's addicted to credit. Cars are leased instead of being purchased. "Buy now, pay later" is a slogan heard from many retailers. And the ultimate move towards credit has been the explosive rise of the credit card!

Prior to the 1950s, credit cards were virtually non-existent. Some stores and businesses would issue credit to their customers to build loyalty, but actual credit cards did not exist. Then in 1949, a fellow by the name of Frank McNamara was dining out with a few friends. When McNamara reached into his pocket to get the cash to pay for the meal, he realized he had forgotten to bring cash. Embarrassed, McNamara got the idea of a "Diner's Club" card – the first credit card. To make a profit (the company did not charge interest), the card charged retailers a 7% fee for accepting the card. In addition, Diner's Club charged cardholders a $3 annual fee. These first cards were made of paper and had the names of the 14 restaurants in New York that accepted the cards printed on the back. The cards were initially targeted to salesmen. Diner's Club grew quickly and had no competition until 1958, when American Express and Bank Americard (later called Visa) came into being.

Today, credit card companies make huge profits from the interest they charge you on your outstanding balance on each of your credit cards. In fact, these companies are banking on the fact that you will overspend and only make the required minimum monthly payments so they can maintain or increase their profits by charging you high interest rates. Many people carry balances on their credit cards and keep racking up these charges. In Canada in 2003, there were over 50 million credit cards in circulation (more than two per adult). Of these, over 22 million cards carried a balance. The total balance outstanding was almost $50 billion. This can be very expensive as it's quite common for credit cards to charge very high interest rates of 20% or more.

Let's use an example to explain. Suppose you decide you want to buy a big plasma TV. You go down to the local electronics store and shell out $3,000 for your chosen TV. You don't have the money to pay for it right now, but you figure you only live once, so you charge it to your credit card – which charges you 18% annual interest. You take the TV home and set it all up.

The next month, your credit card statement arrives and you realize you don't have the money to pay the $3,000 balance off (why would you, you didn't have the money to pay for the TV originally), so you decide to make the minimum payment every month. The minimum required payment varies depending on the credit card company, but let's assume the minimum required payment for your credit card is 2.5% of the outstanding balance every month. Let's take a quick look at 1 year of payments in the chart that follows (if you only make the minimum payment per month):

- In the first month you can see your **Minimum Payment** would be $75.00 (ie. 2.5% is the minimum payment required x $3,000 which is the amount owed) = **$75.00**
  This is the amount in the first column.

- The **Interest Charged** would be **$45.00** ($3,000 x 1.5%). We assumed your credit card company charges a rate of 18% per year which is 1.5% per month (18% per year divided by 12 months). This is the amount in the second column.

- During the first month, you are making a payment of $75, but $45 is the interest charged, so you end up repaying: $75 (payment) − $45 (interest) = **$30 Debt Repaid**

- Since you originally owed $3,000, but you paid $30 off your debt, after one month your balance owing is: $3,000 (amount owed) − $30 (debt repaid) = **$2,970 Balance Owing**
  This is the amount shown in the final column

- During the second month your minimum payment has been reduced to $74.25. This is because: $2,970 (amount owed) x 2.5% (minimum required payment) = **$74.25**

* Note – you can get the calculations for your real life credit card repayments at *www.creditcanada.com/ debtCalc.asp*

Month	Minimum Payment	Interest Charged	Debt Repaid Owing	Balance
NOW				$3,000.00
1	$75.00	$45.00	$30.00	$2,970.00
2	$74.25	$44.55	$29.70	$2,940.30
3	$73.51	$44.10	$29.40	$2,910.90
4	$72.77	$43.66	$29.11	$2,881.79
5	$72.04	$43.23	$28.82	$2,852.97
6	$71.32	$42.79	$28.53	$2,824.44
7	$70.61	$42.37	$28.24	$2,796.20
8	$69.90	$41.94	$27.96	$2,768.23
9	$69.21	$41.52	$27.68	$2,740.55
10	$68.51	$41.11	$27.41	$2,713.15
11	$67.83	$40.70	$27.13	$2,686.01
12	$67.15	$40.29	$26.86	$2,659.15
TOTALS	**$852.10**	**$511.26**	**$340.84**	

After one year of making the minimum payments, you have paid a total of $852.10 on your credit card, but you have only paid off $340.84 of debt! The credit card company receives the other $511.26 you paid in interest.

If you continue making the minimum payments *and never charge anything else to your credit card*, it would take you almost 22 years to completely pay off your debt and you would end up paying $ 4,115 in interest. If it took you 22 years to pay it off, the TV you had bought would be in the garbage long before it had been paid for – and the $3,000 TV becomes a $7,115 TV. Remember, this scenario assumes you never charge anything else to your credit card. In most cases, people who carry a credit card balance do it endlessly as each new purchase that's charged to their card adds to the balance outstanding. Eventually the chains of debt become so heavy that the average wage slave must work just to pay interest. This is the reason you can see so many ads for credit counselling and bankruptcy trustees. It is my opinion that this is a gaping hole in our education system. This should be taught in schools because it is applicable to *virtually everyone.*

Banks love this minimum payment arrangement as they can continually collect huge interest month after month – and earn record profits in the process. Meanwhile, you suffer continual losses of your money. If you want greater financial security (in case your income declines or there is a layoff in your family) and to set out on the road to freedom from financial concern, pay off credit card debts with the highest interest first and do not charge additional items to your cards. Pay the total monthly balance every month – not the minimum required payment.

Tip: Only use credit cards that PAY YOU to use them – AND pay off your balance in full every month!

Seek out credit cards with no membership fees that PAY YOU to use them. For example, one Petro–Canada MasterCard I use offers 2 cents a litre bonus whenever I use the card – which works out to one free week of gas every year. There are other cards, like PC MasterCard which provides 1% in points towards free groceries (that's a free week of groceries every two years). Some banks offer fee-free cards that give you 1% cash back. The simple rule is pay with credit cards for convenience, then pay off your balance in full so you pay no interest, AND collect the free bonuses credit card companies offer. While we're on the subject, I've never understood why debit cards are so popular? In some cases, people are paying fees to use these cards (although some banks offer fee-free debit cards). I understand that there is less risk of

"spending money you don't have", so if that is you, at
least make sure your bank does not charge fees to use
these cards. Another approach is to use a credit card
that *pays YOU a bonus* to use it, and then pay off the card
regularly through online banking.

Going back to the story of the first Diner's Club credit
card – after McNamara founded Diner's Club it grew
quickly and made a profit of $60,000 in its second year.
But McNamara felt it was simply a fad and he sold his
shares in the company to his partners for a little more
than $200,000. Needless to say the whole idea of credit
cards has proven more than a passing fad – and this
shows you how the financial thinking has changed over
the last two generations.

2. Personal/Consumer loans:

Once your credit card debt has been repaid, it's time
to shift your focus to personal loans – which might
include student loans, car loan, lines of credit, or
other consumer loans. By paying these off, you will
further move towards financial independence. Note
that things like car leases (where you are obligated
to pay a fixed amount every month) are also really
consumer loans and should be attacked and elimi-

nated. This also includes furniture or appliances where you pay a small amount every month for years – until it's completely paid off.

Car leasing has become popular over the last number of years and for those with business income there may be certain tax advantages. However, for the average person, leasing is by far the most expensive option for driving a car. To view some comparisons of the cost of leasing versus buying, go to *www.edmunds.com/advice/buying/articles/47079/article.html.* Once again, the main point to remember is that leasing is the most expensive way to drive a car.

I understand that some people want to drive a new car every few years, so if that is important to you then compare the cost of buying the car versus leasing (realizing that at the end of the term when you buy the car you have an asset that you can sell or trade in on your next vehicle). If always driving a newer car is not as important to you, try keeping your current car a little longer. After you have finished making your lease or loan payments, continue making these payments to yourself in a separate savings account so when you are ready to purchase your next vehicle, you have the money set aside to pay cash (or at least a large down payment). If you are currently obligated to make either lease or loan payments for your vehicle, redirecting these payments after you're finished will not be affect your lifestyle – BUT when you are ready to purchase your next vehicle, you will have a large amount of cash to put towards the purchase (so your future debt will be reduced).

Finally try not to fall into the immediate gratification scenario whereby you must purchase items immediately. It's enticing to see a $1,000 item you can buy today and then pay $50 per month for a few years. The problem is that this approach gradually adds to your debt (and interest costs). By saving up first before buying the item, you will save on interest charges (which can be exorbitant) and avoid adding to your debt load.

3. Your Mortgage

For many people, paying of their mortgage is one of the best days of their lives. Once your mortgage is completely paid off, you free up a lot of money for other things. This is a huge step towards breaking the shackles of wage slavery. So how can you do it? From the example about negotiating for a better rate at the beginning of the book, the first step is to rate shop and negotiate with your bank for the best rate you can find. NEVER pay the posted rate at the bank. I would start by looking at the rates offered by the online banks such as PC Financial (*www.pcfinancial.ca*) – then see if your regular bank can beat that rate. Once you've worked to get the best rate possible, you need to concentrate on getting the mortgage paid off as quickly as possible. When I say this, I don't mean that you deny yourself all the things that make life comfortable and worth living – but a little effort can go a long way. The truth is that mortgages are very expensive (which is why the banks seem to report record profits every year). Let's look at this in a little more detail...

Have you ever heard anyone say, "My house is the best investment I ever made." This statement might be true because locking in payments on a mortgage reduces living costs over time (because while rents increase, your outstanding mortgage debt declines). However, people will often think, "I only paid $100,000 for my house and now it's worth $300,000 – so I've tripled my money!" If this example were true, your financial return would be three times your original purchase price. However, not all appears as it seems so let's take a closer look at the TRUE COSTS.

Let's assume you purchased a house 25 years ago for $100,000. You made a $10,000 down payment and took out a mortgage for $90,000 to pay for the balance owing on the home. Your interest rate averaged 8% over the life of your mortgage (remember interest rates are currently at all-time lows, but were much higher during the 80s and 90s). Regardless, under this scenario, you have paid approximately $687 per month for 25 years totalling about $206,000 ($116,000 of which was interest). At the end of this 25-year period, when you add the $10,000 down payment to the $206,000, you have spent a total of $216,000 (over 25 years). In other words, you've really gained:

($300,000 – $216,000) $84,000 over 25 years

This is a far cry from what you originally thought you had gained (i.e. triple your investment). In actual fact, the home is worth around 39% more than the total amount you have paid, NOT the 200% you had originally thought.

I'm not trying to say buying a house is not a good move because in most cases it is, but people often overlook the total amount they *really* paid – because mortgages are expensive and if you had one you did pay for it. How can you make YOUR mortgage less expensive?

Here are a few simple steps you can take:

- research then negotiate for the lowest possible interest rate
- make more frequent payments (such as weekly or bi-weekly)
- pay off a percentage of the principle (make a lump sum payment) every year
- pay an additional amount on each payment (even an extra $20 will help)

Let's take a quick look at these strategies and see how effective they would be using the example shown earlier (i.e. bought a house for $100,000, 25 years ago).

Let's assume you were able to negotiate and thus reduce your average interest rate by half a percent during your mortgage (period of 25 years). In this case your average interest rate would have dropped to 7.5%. Second, you make regular bi-weekly as opposed to monthly mortgage payments. Finally, let's assume you were able to set aside an extra $5 per day to put towards your mortgage as a $1,825 lump sum payment every year. In this situation, your mortgage is fully paid off years earlier and the total amount of money you paid decreases. Instead of paying $116,000 in interest, you now pay only $59,700 – or around half as much. The total cost from the original $216,000 decreases to around $150,000. With this accelerated mortgage payoff strategy, you've doubled your money with your investment. (i.e. your total costs are now around $150,000 and your house is worth $300,000).

The point of this chapter is that there are simple, low-risk ways that you can get out of debt quickly and start on your path to stop working. Remember, getting out of debt should be goal #1 in any financial plan. Now let's move on and look at different sources of income you might have when you stop working – income you might not have fully expected.

4

THE STOP WORKING FORMULA —
THE 4 PIECES OF YOUR
RETIREMENT "PIE"

*"Retirement is like a long vacation
in Las Vegas. The goal is to enjoy
it to the fullest, but not so fully
that you run out of money."*
– Jonathan Clements

Retirement for some people is like sitting down to a nice, warm, freshly baked apple pie (covered with vanilla ice cream if that's your preference). But then the question arises – how can you get that "pie"?

Most people have access to "4 pieces" that they can use to assemble their retirement "pie". The four pieces represent the four sources of income that might be available to you upon retirement. These four sources are:

1. Work-related pension plans (pensions provided by your employer)
2. Government pensions – Canada Pension Plan (CPP), Old Age Security (OAS), and the Guaranteed Income Supplement (GIS)
3. Your home equity if you downsize
4. Personal Savings (RRSPs, Tax-Free Savings Accounts (TSFAs), and other investments)

The optimal situation is if you've managed to create many large pieces to support your income "pie" in retirement. If you are missing some of the pieces, the remaining pieces must be large enough to make up for the smaller or non-existent pieces – or else the size of your pie will shrink. When I decided to leave the workforce at 34, only two of these pieces provided the main foundation to my retirement plan – my house was mortgage-free and I had a fairly sizeable personal financial portfolio which created a comfortable income source. In addition to this I was eligible for some tax credits, but these amounts would not last for the duration of my life. However, I was able to take the leap because I was in my 30s and in the worst–case scenario, I could re–enter the workforce. However, if you are a baby boomer or beyond, you must make sure your pie pieces are as large as possible before you stop working.

This chapter will look at each piece of your retirement pie – so you get a better idea of what income you might expect.

WORK-RELATED PENSION PLANS — THE RETIREMENT HOLY GRAIL (FOR THOSE WHO HAVE ONE)

The difference between having a good employer-sponsored pension plan and not having one is huge. Most people in the public sector have very good "defined-benefit" pension plans along with many other benefits which ensure a pretty comfortable retirement all on their own. In addition, many large companies also offer such plans to their employees (but over time the number of these plans has been shrinking). These days many companies prefer to offer "defined-contribution" plans. I hate boring you with jargon, but the distinction between these types of plans is important – so let's look at these very quickly...

1. Defined-Benefit plans

This is the Cadillac option for employees as the employer "guarantees" a fixed pension payment to the employee for their life. These are generally calculated based on earnings history and years of service. In the public sector, these plans often include a cost of living adjustment so that the recipient does not have to worry about inflation as their income rises as the cost of living goes up. In many cases, people with these types of plans do not have to worry about saving a huge sum of money because their employer-sponsored pension will cover their cost of living.

I vividly remember a presentation I gave regarding investing where one of the attendees came up and chatted with me afterwards. He was interested in hearing my philosophy of investing for his portfolio (and also very interested in dividend reinvestment plans – where the dividends you collect are automatically used to buy more shares – called DRIPs). Since he was an older fellow, I asked him why he would not simply spend his dividends – investing is something you do so you have *money to spend* at some point. He responded that he had worked for the federal government for years and had been pretty frugal and had paid off his house quite young. With his reduced expenses in retirement, he could not even spend his pension income every month. He was actually *still investing more money every month* and he was in his 70s and had been retired for almost a decade. This illustrates the power of having a generous pension plan.

For people who have worked in the private sector, these plans are often not as generous. It is common not to have cost of living increases included which affects benefits. In addition, if the pension plan is under funded (not enough money set aside to meet the obligations of retirees), and the company goes out of business, retirees are left receiving only a fraction of what they might have expected.

I can't get into all these plans in detail because the type of plan you have (if you are fortunate enough to have one) will be unique to your employer. I would encourage you to find out as much as you can about your employer's plan so that you know how much income you can expect from that piece of your retirement "pie". If you do not have a defined benefit plan, you might be part of the increasingly common "defined contribution" plan – so let's take a quick look at those.

2. Defined Contribution plans

Over the last few decades many employers have moved away from the defined *benefit* plans towards defined *contribution* plans. The main reason that companies have moved in this direction is that guaranteeing pensions can be very expensive for employers. If the plans lose money, the employer is forced make additional contributions (out of profits) to top up the pensions. By shifting to defined contribution plans, the risk is shifted to the employees.

Here's a quick overview of how they work. First off there are no guarantees for the employee (and hence no risk for the employer). There are many different plans but a typical arrangement might be that the employee contributes 5% of their salary to the plan and the employer matches that with another 5% – so a total of 10% gets deposited into the plan. This money is invested similarly to how money is invested in an RRSP, and the total amount of money you end up with in your pension plan depends on how the investments perform over time. If you contribute to a pension plan, this will reduce the amount of money you can contribute to an RRSP. However, the recent introduction of Tax-Free Savings Accounts (TSFA) is another avenue available to you – and we'll look at those in a later chapter. Understand that with defined contribution plans, if your investments generate a good rate of return, you end up having a comfortable retirement. If not, you will require other sources of income in order to retire to a comfortable lifestyle. If you are not part of an employer pension plan, the other three pieces of your retirement pie will have to be much larger in order to meet your needs. Now let's continue by looking at the second piece of the pie – universal pension plans offered by the government.

GOVERNMENT PENSIONS (THESE INCLUDE):

- Canada Pension Plan (CPP)
- Old Age Security (OAS)
- Guaranteed Income Supplement (GIS)

One of the retirement pieces of the "pie" that will prove useful to many people is the government funded retirement plans – CPP, OAS, and GIS. Let's take a quick look at them:

1. Canada Pension Plan (CPP):

If you work in Canada, one of the payroll deductions you will notice is CPP. Originally, the CPP was designed to be a "pay as you go" system where current workers contributed money and this money was immediately paid out to current retirees. This system worked well when there were many younger workers supporting fewer older retirees – but then the demographic profile of Canada changed. By the 1990s, it was determined that the plan was unsustainable longer term and actions were taken which included raising the contribution amounts over time to 9.9% (total including employer/employee contributions). This created a pool of assets which could partially pre-fund the plan. In other words, the CPP fund collected more than it spent for retirees (and saved the difference). In addition to this, the government created an investment board to manage the plan's assets – with the hopes of realizing better returns. The end result is that the CPP fund is on pretty stable footing (at least for baby boomers). I still feel younger workers will be contributing more to CPP and getting less in return, but that's an issue for another time.

Basically, if you contributed to CPP, you will be entitled to benefits. The downside is that the CPP is not very generous – the *maximum* benefits for someone retiring at 65 is $908.75 per month ($10,905 per year in 2009). This maximum benefit is based on an income level of $46,300 or more (if you earn less than this amount, you will collect less in CPP benefits). However, a good point is that CPP pension benefits are indexed to the government-calculated "consumer prices index (CPI)" – which measures general prices. So the amount you will receive does increase every year with inflation to some degree.

To get an idea of how much you will be entitled to in less than 5 minutes, simply call CPP at 1–800–277–9914 and ask for an estimate of how much you can expect to receive based on your historical contributions. The closer you are to retirement, the more accurate the number you get will be.

One other thing worth noting is that you can collect CPP at age 60 instead of age 65, however you will be penalized 0.5% per month. In other words, someone deciding to take CPP at age 60 instead of 65 would get (0.5% x (12 months per year) x (5 years) = 30% less than their regular entitlement. Similarly, if you defer taking the pension, you will get an additional 0.5% per month up to age 70 (30% more). It's worth noting that these rules are set to change in the next few years and the penalty for early pension recipients will become 0.6% per month and the bonus for taking the pension later will be 0.7% per month.

Overall, the main point to remember is that CPP is not very generous, but it is fairly dependable (for boomers at least). For younger people, the plan will still be there for them, but depending on future investment performance it might become a little less generous either with monthly benefit amounts or with the age at which people are entitled to start collecting.

2. Old Age Security (OAS):

OAS is paid based on having lived in Canada – work history is irrelevant. The only criteria required to receive OAS is you must have been a resident of Canada for at least 10 years and have reached the age of 65. In order to get the maximum benefit, you must have a total of 40 years of residence in Canada. For every year less than 40, your benefit is reduced on a pro-rated basis. The maximum benefit is $516.96

per month. This benefit is paid out of government revenues, so if the government goes back into deficits, they will begin to look at either raising taxes or cutting benefits. However, with a mass of boomers set to start benefiting from these programs, any government that wants to win elections will have to tread carefully in this area.

This benefit is clawed back at a rate of $0.15 for every dollar of net income over $66,335. In addition, this income is treated as regular income and taxes are paid on it based on your income level.

3. Guaranteed Income Supplement (GIS):

If you are eligible for OAS, you might also be eligible for GIS. This is based on very low income levels and must be applied for every year. Most people will not be eligible for this benefit. For additional information, check the following website:

http://www.rhdcc-hrsdc.gc.ca/eng/isp/oas/oastoc.shtml

This site has all the information you need relating to OAS. Note that income you receive from OAS does not count as income for GIS.

Now that we've looked at your government pension, let's move onto your house and see how it might be able to provide you with some additional income.

YOUR HOUSE — HOW CAN IT HELP YOU RETIRE?

Owning a home is the largest investment most people ever make in their lives, but do you need this home for life? By purchasing a home, you've locked in a large portion of your living expenses and signed up for a forced savings plan by gradually paying down a mortgage. This is a crucial piece of the retirement puzzle which is one of the reasons that I mentioned it in my first book. Paying off your mortgage is one of the great risk–free, tax–free investments you can make. When you're approaching retirement, there is a way to use your house to unlock some wealth and boost your retirement lifestyle. I will give you an example of two older couples I know who have done just that.

Leaving the "burbs" for...

1. A small town

I know of a couple who moved away from the suburbs and out to a small town about 30 minutes from the city. This town of approximately 15,000 people had the amenities they sought – nature, parks, restaurants, shops, a fitness centre, fresh air, and a local hospital. This move happened a few years ago. The move was to a reasonably-sized bungalow.

Let's take a quick look at the financial impact of this move. I will offer an estimate of the financial results as I don't know all the real-life figures, but the general idea is what's important. First, the price difference between the big house in the suburbs (valued at $395,000) and the smaller bungalow in the small town ($195,000) instantly created $200,000 of usable cash which could be deposited into an investment account. In addition to these savings – by moving into a smaller house, the taxes, maintenance, and utilities expenses decreased by around $2,000 per year. If the couple invested the $200,000 and earned 5% per year, they instantly created an extra ($200,000 @5%) $10,000 per year. With the $2,000 in savings they received by maintaining a smaller home, they have created an extra $12,000 per year in disposable income (not to mention the reduced time and energy needed for upkeep).

2. The Downtown Condo

Another couple I know sold their house and moved into a downtown condo. They liked the easy access to all the services offered and maintenance-free lifestyle. They did end up getting a fairly large amount of money to invest because the cost of the condo was less than their house, but their overall monthly expenses increased due to the high cost of condo fees. However, they no longer needed two cars and they found they could walk to most destinations. This has pretty much offset the extra condo fees (and they've boosted their nest-egg with the proceeds from their house).

Selling your house can quickly put a fairly substantial chunk of extra money in your pocket if you are at that stage in life. This trend of downsizing should pick up over time as baby boomers get older. If you are younger and still need the large house for comfort because you have a family (like me) – then at least concentrate on paying the mortgage down as quickly as possible.

YOUR PERSONAL SAVINGS
(RRSPS, TSFAS, AND OTHER MONEY)

The remainder of the book focuses on various types of personal savings. The idea is to see how much you will earn from your first three pieces of the "pie" – then you know how big your investment accounts, the fourth piece, must be. In many cases, you probably won't need to save millions to retire or take undue risks to reach your goals. Some people might not have to really save at all (if they will have good defined pensions), while others will have to save much more (people without pensions). Before we get into some little-known, low-risk investing strategies for your savings, let's take a look at a fictional couple in their 50s who have not saved a penny and see how they might fair when they stop working.

5

YOU MAY BE RICHER THAN YOU THINK

*"When a man's stomach is full,
it makes no difference whether
he is rich or poor."*
– Euripides

MEET "THE SPENDTHRIFTS" — (A FICTIONAL COUPLE):
Let's look at a hypothetical couple in their 50s who are
established in their careers and plan on retiring at age
65 (in a little more than 10 years). Neither has the benefit of a company pension plan. Both spouses work and
earn $50,000 each per year (reasonable but not outrageous
salaries). They pay their mortgage every month and then
spend the remaining amount. They never save *anything* in

RRSPs or other investment accounts. Their only major asset is their house.

Let's do a brief comparison with their working income now and their income after they retire – *on an after-tax basis* (net income) for comparison. We'll assume they own a home valued at $350,000 which cost them $175,000 to purchase 20 years ago. They are near the end of their mortgage payments on their $150,000 mortgage which currently is a fixed 5–year mortgage at 4%. They also have work–related expenses of $200 each per month. This could include parking costs, transit fares, union/professional dues, cost of lunches, dry–cleaning expenses,...

Here's their income after taxes and mortgage payments:

1. Now:

Two people earning $50,000 each of gross income:

	Husband	Wife
Salary	$ 50,000	$ 50,000
Less: (Income taxes)	–(9,860)	–(9,860)
Less: CPP premiums	–(2,049)	–(2,049)
Less: EI premiums	–(711)	–(711)
After-tax Income:	$ 37,380	$ 37,380

Less: Working Expenses	–(2,400)	–(2,400)
Real Take-Home Income	$ 34,980	$ 34,980
Family Income (2 x 34,980)	$ 69,960	
Less: Mortgage ($150K@4%, 25yrs)	–(9,468)	

Disposable Income $60,492 (or around $5,000 per month)

2. After Retirement:

The *same couple* with NO investment savings, RRSPs, or company pension plans. Their ONLY source of income in retirement will be CPP and OAS (along with a few meagre tax credits. However, they are now mortgage–free.

	Husband	**Wife**
CPP	$10,905	$10,905
OAS (old age security)	$ 6,204	$ 6,204
Less: (Income taxes)	–(440)	–(440)
Less: CPP premiums	– nil –	– nil –
Less: EI premiums	– nil –	– nil –
After-tax Income:	$16,669	$16,669
Less: Working Expenses	– nil –	– nil –
Real Take-Home Income	$16,669	$16,669
Family Income (2 x 16,669)	$33,338	
Less: Mortgage (now paid off)	– nil –	

Add: Provincial Tax Credits	$	678
Add: Ont. Seniors Property Grant	$	250
Add: GST credit	$	401
Disposable Income	**$34,667**	
(or almost $2,900 per month)		

Notice how they only earn about 33% *before tax* of what they were earning while working, BUT their *after-tax* and after expense income is almost 60% of what they were earning while working. Taxes are the biggest costs most people face. This is the structure of our income tax system in retirement – which tends to be pretty generous towards retired people. However, this is a *POSSIBLE worst-case scenario* of an example couple who never saved a penny for retirement. This is not a model to try to emulate, but it just shows a possible situation without any retirement planning or savings (or company pension plans). Although this couple could be more comfortable, they are not destined to eating cat food and seeking shelter in a cardboard box. With their house paid off, their basic living costs should be quite low.

One important point that is often brought up at this point is health care. In Canada, visiting a doctor and all emergency services are covered through our taxes. These health services are accessible to anyone with a health card. It's also important to note that many provinces also offer drug plans to their residents. In Ontario for example, they have the "Ontario Drug Benefit Program". With this plan, senior couples earning above $24,175 combined (which is the case with this fictional couple) would pay a $100 deductible per person per year. After the deductible is paid, they would only be asked to pay a dispensing fee of up to $6.11 per filled prescription.

You must realize that as you get older, you will rely on the health care system more frequently. Dentures, eyeglasses, canes, walkers, etc can be expensive and you should budget for them. Overall, we are lucky that we live in a country that covers a portion of your health needs, but planning for these potential costs is prudent. If you are getting close to stop working, check for information about what plans if any are offered by your province. Knowing how much and what requirements your provincial plan will fund is important. Some provinces such as Ontario have an "assisted devices" program that you must apply for. This program covers partial costs of some medical devices.

So in this first example, we assumed that this couple spent *every last cent they earned while working –*

without *any* savings for retirement. Regardless, although they would not have a huge income, they also wouldn't be destined for complete poverty. Let's continue with this fictional couple and make a few small changes...

SMALL CHANGES — BIG RESULTS!

Would you be happy with just 60% of your pre-retirement disposable income? I wouldn't. Let's suppose this couple is not happy with only having about 60% of their disposable income in retirement. Let's make a couple of small changes to their situation to boost their income. We'll still assume they don't have any company pension plans and have not accumulated any savings for retirement. In addition, we don't want to affect their standard of living one iota while they're working – they don't want to sacrifice that area of their life. Let's simply make the following two small changes:

1. Once their mortgage is fully paid off, redirect the same monthly "mortgage" amount into a new investment account such as an RRSP or the new TSFA (tax-free savings account) every year until they retire.

2. Downsize to a smaller, less expensive house upon retirement.

There is a chapter dedicated to tax-free savings accounts (TSFAs) a little later in the book, but let's take a quick look at RRSPs. An RRSP is not in itself an investment, but instead a certain kind of account which offers certain tax benefits. When you contribute to an RRSP, the government will give you some of the money you contributed back through a tax refund (one of the key benefits of an RRSP). In addition, any investments held within an RRSP can grow without being taxed. The only time you pay tax on money in your RRSP is when you take it out.

How would these two small changes affect our fictional couple in retirement? First, by redirecting their former mortgage payments into a savings account once their mortgage is paid off, they would not affect their current lifestyle because they would still have the same amount of disposable income to spend. Since their mortgage payment amounts to around $9,500 (as shown in the first chart earlier), they would accumulate almost $9,500 in savings every year (we'll assume for 10 years). For our example, we'll assume they put this money into an RRSP. Assuming they earn 5% per year, after 10 years they would have accumulated approximately:

$9,500 per year for 10 years invested @ 5% = $125,000.

Realize that because they put their mortgage savings into an RRSP, they would get a tax refund every year of approximately 31% of what they contributed (at their income level). So:

$9,500 x 31% = $2,945

Once again, we're assuming that the couple doesn't want to alter their current lifestyle after they pay off the mortgage, so they don't need this extra money. They could therefore save it in their tax-free savings account (TSFA). With the same return of 5% per year, they would have another:

$2,945 per year for 10 years invested @ 5% = $38,000

They would have another $38,000 tucked away in their TSFA with this one simple move.

If they could keep earning 5% per year on both their RRSP and their TSFA after they retire, they would earn an extra:

RRSP ($125,000 X 5%) = $ 6,250
Less: Income Taxes   -(1,312)
Extra Income $ 4,938
TSFA ($38,000 X 5%) = $ 1,900

Less: Income Taxes – nil –

RESULT: Extra Income $ 6,838

Realize that they would earn this extra income for as long as they live.

The second step would involve selling their larger suburban house (the one they raised their children in) and moving to a smaller, less costly house such as a bungalow (without the hassles of stairs) or to a condo apartment. The type of move would depend on the lifestyle they wanted, but either move could potentially free up cash for them. Let's assume they move into a bungalow which costs around $250,000. Since their current larger suburban home is valued at $350,000, the bungalow is around $100,000 less expensive. So from this move, they instantly generate a windfall $100,000 (which is tax-free because it's a principle residence).

Let's assume they can invest this extra $100,000 in their TSFA. In this case, if they earn 5% per year on their $100,000, they would create an extra:

($100,000@5%) = **$5,000 per year *tax-free!***

RESULT: Extra Income of $5,000

Downsizing inherently means reduced costs such as property taxes and general upkeep. A reasonable estimate (based on a comparison I made with two houses fitting this scenario) would generate the following savings:

$1,000 per year in property taxes

$500 per year in decreased maintenance costs

$500 per year in decreased heat/electricity costs

RESULT: Savings of $2,000

These two small changes would create extra annual income (as shown above). If we add the three numbers from the savings (from above), we get:

RRSP/TSFA savings	$ 6,838
Home downsizing	$ 5,000
Reduced home expenses	$ 2,000
Total Extra Income	**$13,838**

With the $34,667 this couple could originally expect to earn from CPP and OAS, the extra $13,838 they could realize in savings from these two small adjustments would increase their *net* income to $48,505 per year. Remember right now by working, they earn around $60,482 *net*. So **by never saving one red cent for the first 50-plus years of their lives**, they are able to earn around $4,000 per month after they retire (instead of $5,000 per month working) **without having an employer sponsored pension plan.**

Another point to consider is that after working all their lives, a lot of people prefer to slow down, but not stop working completely. A good portion of retirees seek part-time employment. For this couple, part-time employment would bridge this income gap. This can be an option for some people – but you should only pursue working if you enjoy it.

Remember this is not a model to emulate, but a quick look at a couple who had not saved one penny towards retirement until well into their 50s. This example may be applicable to your own personal financial situation or provide you with a basic financial outline. The point is that even without saving anything, people may already have a lot more income than they realize!

The remainder of this book will let you in on some of the secrets that some financial experts might not want you to know. There are many ways you can invest to reach your goals – but let's first take a look at your retirement "pie".

6

MAKING YOUR RETIREMENT "PIE"

*"I'm retired — goodbye tension,
hello pension!"*
– Author Unknown

Now that we have looked at a fictional couple, you can use that example as a rough guide to figure out what *you* need to do to stop working. The closer you are reaching retirement, the more accurate your figures will be. If you are a long way away from retiring from the work force, you can still make a rough plan and then revisit it every year to see if you need to make any adjustments.

Let's start with the path I took just to help illustrate the general idea. Even though I decided to leave the rat race at 34, I had to do similar calculations that every aspiring retiree must do BUT with one exception. I had to rely on one huge piece of the retirement "pie" – income from my financial portfolio.

Since I was living off the income generated from my portfolio, my biggest risk was that the income would not grow as fast as inflation over the long-term (and long-term could be more than half a century). My approach (which probably would not be suitable for most older people) was to concentrate exclusively on dividend-paying stocks (stocks which paid me some money regularly out of their profits). The idea is that even as prices rise over time, the companies that are providing these same products or services also raise the prices of their goods or services, which means they earn more profit – and then are in the position to raise the dividends to shareholders like myself. My major retirement commandment was to NEVER spend my capital (the money that was in my portfolio) – only spend the income my stocks generated.

Six years on, this strategy has worked reasonably well. Many established companies have long histories of increasing dividends much faster than inflation – and hence the stockholder becomes richer over time. The main reason I was so comfortable with having my portfolio in dividend-paying stocks is that my house was fully paid and I had no other debt when I took the plunge and stopped working at such an early age. History has shown that although dividend investing can be volatile at times – overall it's been very rewarding. The second reason I felt confident leaving the rat race is that I was still in my 30s so if my dividend-paying stocks couldn't support my lifestyle, I could always re-enter the workforce as an educated professional.

One reason I was able to become financially free is that throughout my youth and 20s I chose not to accumulate material items. Even when backpacking in Europe and Asia, I only purchased items I could physically carry in my backpack. This simple lifestyle was enriching as I was able to see parts of the world while also being able to save money to invest. It's amazing how much you can save on a small income when you are not encountering all the expenses of day-to-day life. During this time I was also able to minimize my payable taxes as I could contribute to an RRSP in years where I was gainfully employed (and thus save on taxes), and then withdraw it in years when my income was much lower – such as when I was travelling.

But you might not be in the same situation – so you must take a look at things from *your* perspective. The nice thing about retiring is that a lot of the expenses you incur while working (i.e. child care, commuting costs, work-related wardrobe) simply "disappear". Once you stop working, your taxes go down, you stop paying CPP, EI , and other work-related deductions. In addition to this, you also stop saving for retirement because you're already retired! You may also be in the position to downsize if your kids are gone (in fact you might want to do that quickly before your kids decide to move back home, which is a recent trend)! You will also receive more income from either government pension plans or your own work-related pension plans – something I could not rely on.

The downside you might face if you are planning to retire at an older age than I did is that you might not want to take on as much risk as I did. You might choose a more conservative portfolio and accept the probability of earning less money on your investments in exchange for not having to worry. That's what this book is going to do for you – give you some conservative strategies that will allow you to reduce your risk without reducing your potential investment returns too much. The investment part of your retirement "piece of the pie" should be managed carefully, and hopefully you can use some of the ideas I outline in the following chapters.

The decision is yours, the power is yours and the strategies are relatively simple. I started investing because I had the extra money at the time and everyone was being bombarded with information about RRSPs, mutual funds, and investing around the time I was attending university. I graduated during the recession in the early 1990s and could only obtain minimum-paying jobs at that time. So I decided to travel and see the world while still saving up and investing. I didn't have a concrete plan – just a feeling that if I was continually investing while travelling, that I would be wealthy at some point while also having spent my 20s having fun. It wasn't until much later that I realized I might be able to stop working at an early age.

You however need a plan now in order to reach your goals. You can take a look at some retirement planning books such as *"The Pension Puzzle" by Bruce Cohen and Brian Fitzgerald or "The New Retirement" by Sherry Cooper* for information. However, let's start by giving you a basic framework. Realize this is simply a rough guide and there may be more factors you might consider.

Here are some essential steps you should follow:

1. Rid yourself of all debt (this includes credit cards, personal loans, your mortgage, and also any quasi debt such as car leases. Wherever

possible, buy the asset instead of agreeing to a contract that steals wealth from you on a regular basis – which is what leases do to you.

2. Calculate how much income you will need to live on in retirement (after tax). Remember to include costs you might not have now such as new hobbies, travelling costs, and possible medical expenses.

3. Calculate how much you expect to receive (for you and your spouse) from work-related pension plans and government plans (such as CPP, OAS) if you are at that age. You might want to either take your CPP early or late (this affects how much money the government will ultimately pay you). In making the decision on when to start collecting CPP, you have to determine what's best for you.

4. Calculate the difference between how much you need to live on in #2 with how much you can expect in #3. If you are really lucky, the amount you expect to earn will be more than the amount you expect you'll need. If the opposite is true (you will earn less than you need in retirement to live the lifestyle you want), you will need to increase your income through other means.

5. Determine any savings (RRSPs, TSFAs, and personal accounts) that you might have. Don't panic if you haven't saved as much as you would have liked – you can often still reach your goals really quickly as we saw with the "Spendthrifts" – the fictional couple in the last chapter.

6. Determine how much income your current investments in #5 will generate. You should do this calculation using conservative numbers (assume you will earn a fairly low rate of return to give you a margin of safety. (Ex. 4%)

7. Calculate: Take the amount in #4 (the extra amount you think you need after pension income) and subtract the amount in #6 (how much you expect your investments to earn every year). If you determine that you will have enough income to live the lifestyle you want, you should be okay in retirement. If not, you need to plan for some other income–generating ideas to bridge the income gap you will face in retirement. This can include saving and investing more for retirement, considering working part–time, downsizing, or selling material items you no longer need such as boats, trailers, motorcycles, or any extra unused vehicles.

The aim of this book is to give you a basic outline of how you might manage to reach your stop working goals. It is impossible to give an absolute plan as everyone's situation will be different. However the above outline offers a general guide that you can use to begin planning for your retirement.

Finally, once you have a basic plan in place, you have to get your portfolio on track to give you the income you'll need to retire comfortably. That is the purpose of this book – to offer you investing options that should allow you to earn more from your investments without taking on more risk. These strategies might not be widely advertised because in some cases you earn more *because* the financial industry earns less – so it's not in their best interest.

Let's start our journey with a look at the foundation of many investment portfolios – the stock market. We'll start with a simple strategy that will allow you to assemble a financial portfolio that you can manage in less than one hour per year.

7

USING THE "15-MINUTE PORTFOLIO" TO DOUBLE YOUR WEALTH

"Simplicity is the ultimate sophistication."
– Leonardo da Vinci

I wrote my second book, *"The Lazy Investor"*, to demonstrate to those individuals who may have small sums of money how to invest these amounts more efficiently. This strategy is straightforward and effortless once it's all set up and is a very effective method for building wealth over time. The most important point in *"The Lazy Investor"* was that it showed you how to avoid the financial fees you (the investor) face. By avoiding these fees, you keep the original sums of money in your pocket while continuing to reinvest it to create your own wealth.

The point of avoiding fees may sound unimportant, but it is this attention to financial detail that gives you the power to conserve these small sums and make your money work for YOU. I will elaborate on this point from a personal perspective.

Have you ever dined at the CN Tower Restaurant in Toronto? It is a wonderful experience and well worth the cost. You are dining above the clouds – 1,000 feet above the ground while the restaurant slowly revolves 360 degrees. It takes 72 minutes to complete one rotation. As it slowly revolves, you are you are enjoying the Toronto skyline as well as Lake Ontario.

While dining there I noticed that one of the more prominent features of the Toronto skyline were huge signs atop various buildings – mostly Canada's big banks. While exploring the Toronto downtown, I noticed numerous other buildings displaying signs from Canada's other major financial companies along Bay Street. The question that came to mind was how can the financial industry afford so much office space adorned with massive signs in these prime buildings? After all, these companies do not produce tangible goods yet they earn huge profits.

Let's take a look at one way money is earned by the financial industry – starting with mutual funds. However, rather than looking at it from the company's perspective, let's look at it from your perspective – as an investor. I'll use a fictional example to show you how expensive these seemingly innocent fees can be (we'll ignore taxes for now to keep things simple).

Let's assume two 20–year–old twin brothers are left an inheritance of $100,000 each. They decide to invest the money for the next 35 years in the hopes of retiring by age 55. The first brother decides to invest in mutual funds. These mutual funds earn 10% per year over 35 years (before expenses). However, the mutual fund company charges 2.5% management fees. Many people don't realize that this 2.5% is charged to them because it is taken directly out of the fund **before** you see the fund results. Therefore, the **actual** return for this brother is (10% – 2.5%) = 7.5% per year after expenses. At the end of 35 years, the first brother checks his statements to see how much his investments have grown to. He finds that his $100,000 has grown to an impressive:

$100,000 invested @ 7.5% (net) for 35 years =
approx $1,157,000

The second brother invests in exchange-traded funds (ETFs – which I will explain a little later) which we'll assume incur a small average fee of 0.25%. If we assume his investments earn the same 10% per year as his brother, his net return is (10% – 0.25%) = 9.75%. At the end of 35 years, he too looks at how his investments have performed over time and finds:

$100,000 invested @ 9.75% (net) for 35 years =

approx $2,495,000

By avoiding a large percentage of the fees the mutual fund company charges (i.e. 0.25% instead of 2.5%), the second brother has managed to earn more than double what the first brother did ($2.49 million versus $1.15 million)! By minimizing the usual 2.5% fee many stock mutual fund investors pay – the second brother becomes much wealthier.

I am constantly amazed at the number of amateur investors who blindly hand over their money to mutual fund companies to manage. Historically, investors (like you and me) have been told that investing is too complicated for the average person to understand – with financial jargon, detailed tables and mathematical calculations. The message has been that if you buy the professionally managed funds your financial return will be much better than if you try to manage your portfolio by yourself. This begs my first question: "Did your professionally managed mutual funds not lose money during the stock market crash in late 2008?"

The reality is that the majority of mutual funds lost a tremendous amount of money. That doesn't mean the managers were inept because virtually every stock investor lost money during this time. However there is a point to be driven home here and that is while mutual fund investors (like you or I) lost up to 50% of the money they had invested in the stock market, the mutual fund companies continued collecting their 2–3% or more in management fees during this same period. Not once did I see a headline stating, "Due to difficult market conditions and massive investor losses, we are waiving our fees for this year." In other words, even though **you took all the risk and lost money, mutual fund companies kept collecting *their* money**. This system is such that if you win (ie. your investments provide you with a large return), the mutual companies also win (because the fees will also increase with higher returns). However, **if you lose, they *still* win**. Currently there are hundreds of billions of dollars invested in mutual funds in Canada – sometimes earning money for the investors (but always earning fees for the financial companies who control them). Let me explain using a couple of everyday examples to drive home the point that *small sums of money do count (and should be saved to reinvest)*.

When I was a kid, it was very common for drivers to have the option of going to "full-serve" gas stations where the workers would fill your tank for you or "self-serve" stations where you filled the tank yourself. The self-serve stations were a few cents a gallon cheaper (at that time Canada used gallons), but these savings motivated people to get out of their cars to fill them up themselves. More recently countless home owners have flocked to home renovation stores such as The Home Depot to do their own home repairs in order to save money on labour costs. People are willing to try these home projects they have never done before because they want to save a large portion of the costs – the labour. Can you, the investor, apply the same principle to your financial portfolio? Yes you can.

What can you do to earn more money – *without* having to read and negotiate complex financial jargon regarding investing? Perhaps you lack confidence in your abilities to manage and invest your money on your own or you don't have an interest in this subject. You may wonder how you, Mr/Mrs "Average" person could earn the same financial returns that expert or professional stock pickers earn.

STOP! I want to reassure you that this is not as daunting as it seems. The truth is that the vast majority of mutual funds managed by professional money managers fail to perform as well as the markets they're invested in. This sounds strange at first, but if you think about it you'll quickly realize this has to be the case. Let's look at a quick analogy to explain:

If you have ever been to a major sporting event, you might not have a perfect view of the playing field or surface from where you are seated. There are other spectators who might be obstructing your view so how can you get a better view of the game? You can simply stand up and get a perfectly clear view of everything that's going on. This simple manoeuvre works wonderfully! Let's take this a step further.

What if everyone stands up to get a better view? If you can see better when you stand up, it makes sense that everyone can see better if they all stand up – right? Of course not! If only a few people stand up, they can get a better view and the manoeuvre works perfectly, but if everyone stands up, you're back to where you started because then everyone has an obstructed view once again.

This scenario can be applied to professional money management. If the stock markets were flooded with novice investors (average people like you and me) who made up the majority of the stock market, then the few professional money managers with their army of stock market analysts would be able to find superior investments that earn very high returns – that we amateur investors would have probably overlooked. But once a large percentage of the money invested in stock markets is controlled by professional money managers (as is the case right now in major stock markets), these opportunities to gain extra profit are greatly reduced and can actually disappear. This is because if there is a great stock that has a bright future and the price the stock is a steal of a deal, the professional money managers quickly discover it and buy it. This increases the price of the stock – making it not such a great bargain any longer. This is why if you look at the various mutual fund money managers, *the vast majority of them* do not create returns higher than the stock market over the long term. This means that if you as an amateur investor bought all the stocks in the stock market, you would earn the same or similar returns as the professional money managers.

My investment strategy has been to buy quality dividend-paying companies that offer essential products or services (such Enbridge (home heating), Johnson and Johnson (healthcare), or Kraft (food)) and collect the dividends. The key is avoiding the fees and collecting *all* the rewards – which can be a huge factor as we saw at the beginning of the chapter with the two fictional brothers. My approach has worked very well for me.

However, many people don't feel confident buying stocks on their own. Others don't have the time or interest to choose individual stocks. If this sounds like you, what can you do?

The answer may be to consider buying index funds or exchange traded funds (ETFs) as opposed to buying various mutual funds. At this point, you may feel confused, thinking, "What's this guy talking about?", so I'll explain this idea in basic English.

Index funds are a special type of mutual fund. What's the difference between index funds and mutual funds? First, instead of paying a professional mutual fund manager to *choose* stocks (to try to add value for investors), the index fund mechanically invests money into all the stocks on a major stock market index. For example, in Canada, rather than a mutual fund manager choosing which bank stocks to buy, the index fund would buy a little of every one of them. Second, the difference between regular mutual funds and index funds are the fees that are charged to average investors (like you and me). Index funds charge much less in fees than mutual funds managed by professional money managers. Many index funds may charge fees of less than 0.5% while mutual funds often charge 2.5% or more.

Here are the words from Warren Buffett, arguably the world's greatest billionaire investor on May 6, 2007 – one day after his corporation's annual meeting discussing index investing:

> "A very low-cost index is going to beat a majority of the amateur-managed money or professionally-managed money… The gross performance may be reasonably decent, but **the fees will eat up a significant percentage of the returns**," he said. "You'll pay lots of fees to people who do well, and lots of fees to people who do not do so well."

In other words what he is saying is that by avoiding the fees, you will earn more money. He has no vested interest in saying this, so there would be no incentive for him to "sell" this idea to people if he didn't truly believe it.

As stated earlier, exchange traded funds (ETFs) are very similar to index funds in that investors in these products are charged low fees and the ETFs are mechanically invested into many different stocks. The difference with ETFs is that if you want to invest in them you must buy them through a brokerage account and you will incur small brokerage commissions to buy them (between $10 to $30 depending on the size of your account). The advantage is that the ongoing management fees of ETFs are often even lower than with many index funds. You can set up a **discount** brokerage account at any major bank in Canada – and they will open this account for free. Just walk in (or call) your bank and tell them you'd like to open a discount brokerage account and they will guide you through the whole process. Once your account is opened, you can buy ETFs (or many index funds) quickly.

Right now you might be wondering which is better – ETFs or Index funds? The answer depends, but here's a simple rule of thumb to guide you:

If you are starting with a small amount of money and plan to invest a small amount periodically (ex. $200 per month), then index funds would be more suitable because you will not incur trading fees to buy them.

If you have a larger amount of money to invest (at least $25,000) and only plan on adding additional money to your portfolio occasionally (perhaps once a year or less often), then ETFs might be better than index funds. The reason this is the case is because although you will pay brokerage fees to buy the ETFs (around $10 to $30 each time), your ongoing management fees with ETFs will be even lower than with index funds, so overall you will save money.

A very good example of this low-fee approach to investing is a strategy explained in *Moneysense* magazine. The magazine calls it the "couch potato" portfolio and you can get a quick run-down of the whole process by Googling "Moneysense Couch Potato". After the Moneysense page appears, scroll down and click on the box entitled, "Couch Potato Portfolio". There you can read an article and also click on a few other links related to this strategy. The idea is that you can set up a portfolio in less than 15 minutes a year and it will create better investment returns than the vast majority of regular mutual funds **because the fees are so much lower than those charged by the average mutual fund company.**

Let's take a quick look at how this would work for two different types of investors:

1. An investor who is contributing small amounts every month (ex. $200/month)
2. An investor who already has a larger investment portfolio (at least $25,000)

1. The "monthly contribution" investor:

If you are trying to build wealth through regular monthly investments, then buying index funds might be the best option as you will avoid the brokerage fees. Here's how to start this plan:

1. Open a discount brokerage account
2. Invest in a group of index funds (no commissions on many of these)
3. Rebalance once a year

Let's briefly walk you through the process. As I mentioned earlier, you can open up a *discount* brokerage account at any major bank and the bank employees can walk you through the process – and there should be no cost for this. We'll use TD Waterhouse (the discount broker for TD Canada Trust) as an example because that is the company I am most familiar with and they offer competitive (ie. low-fee) index funds. If you want to start off with a simple portfolio that is pretty well-diversified (and charges low fees), you might decide to put $100 per month into each of the following funds:

• TD Canadian Index Fund

- TD US Index Fund
- TD International Index Fund
- TD Canadian Bond Fund

*Note: These index funds are called the TD "e-series" funds because they are purchased online through your discount brokerage account. If you don't know how to buy these funds through your brokerage account, call the broker and ask them to give you step-by-step instructions on the process (they should do this at no cost).

Another factor you might want to consider is that generally bond funds offer lower investment returns than stock funds (over the long term) but they are considered to be more conservative investments because your money is more secure (or virtually guaranteed in the case of government bonds). Usually, the older you get, the more money you may want to invest in more conservative investments such as bonds. A general rule of thumb is to allocate the percentage to the bond fund equal to your age. So if you are 40 years old, you might want to put 40% of your money into the bond fund and then divide the remaining 60% of your money equally into the other three funds (20% in each). This rule is not cast in stone, but it offers a rough idea on how you may want to invest your money. If you invest too much money into bonds when you are younger, you run the risk of your money no growing as fast as inflation over time. Even older investors should have some exposure to stocks for this reason.

Let's assume you invest in a group of index funds allocating $400 per month equally among the four funds (this means you invest $100 into each of the four funds every month). You do this automatically for a year. At the end of the year, some investments have increased in value while others have declined. Let's assume that your portfolio looked like this at the end of the year (where two investments have increased in value while two investments declined):

- $1,100 invested in TD Canadian Index Fund
- $1,500 invested in TD US Index Fund
- $1,500 invested in TD International Index Fund
- $1,100 invested in TD Canadian Bond Fund

This is where you focus on rebalancing your portfolio to move it back to approximate your original allocation (25% invested in each fund). From the example portfolio above, your total portfolio is now worth $5,200. If your goal is to put 25% in each index fund, you would want to make sure you have $1,300 in each one. Therefore, you would remove $200 from each of the TD US Index fund and the TD International Index Fund and add $200 to both the TD Canadian Index Fund and the TD Canadian Bond Fund. Once you've done this (rebalanced), your portfolio would look like this (with 25% of your money invested in each fund:

- $1,300 invested in TD Canadian Index Fund
- $1,300 invested in TD US Index Fund
- $1,300 invested in TD International Index Fund
- $1,300 invested in TD Canadian Bond Fund

Once you've done this you can keep investing $100 per month into each of the index funds for another year. In a year's time, rebalance once again (ensuring approximately 25% of your portfolio is in each fund).

2. The Investor already with a large portfolio

The idea is similar if you already have a large portfolio (at least $25,000). Once you have your brokerage account set up, you can buy various ETFs. Your broker can explain how to place the order, but here are some examples from the portfolio *Moneysense Magazine* uses:

1. iShares Canadian   – (this invests in
   Composite Index   Canadian stocks)
2. iShares S&P 500   – (this invests in US
   Index   stocks)
3. iShares MSCI EAFE   – (this invests in
   Index   international stocks)
4. iShares Canadian   – (this invests in bonds)
   Bond Index Fund

Although you might choose a different combination of ETFs for your portfolio, let's look at the "couch potato" strategy to gain a better understanding of how it works. The "couch potato" strategy invests 20% of your money in each of the first three ETFs (totalling 60%) and then 40% in the bond fund to give you a fairly good mix of investments. Some investors might want to put 25% in each of the four ETFs or invest some other amount in each. The percentage you invest into each fund would depend on your own personal situation and how much risk you're willing to take (remember stocks are generally more risky than bonds in the shorter term) but have historically offered better returns.

After you've implemented this strategy and decided which funds you want to invest in, you simply check it once a year and keep the percentages the same as when you first set the strategy up. So for example, let's start with a sample portfolio that uses the above mix of funds with an equal 25% of your money invested into each of the four ETFs (above). Let's assume you originally invested $50,000. In this scenario, your starting portfolio would look like this:

Fund	Amount
iShares Canadian Composite Index	$ 12,500
iShares S&P 500 Index	$ 12,500
iShares MSCI EAFE Index	$ 12,500
iShares Canadian Bond Index Fund	$ 12,500
Total Portfolio	**$50,000**

After one year you realize some funds had earned a better return than others (which will almost always happen). Perhaps the Canadian stock market increased more than the US stock market or bonds earned more money than stocks. If this happens you would add money to the investments that performed poorly and/or remove money from the investment that had done well. Let's use a simple example to explain this. Suppose your portfolio had merely gained 2%, but Canadian stocks and bonds had outperformed other investments such that your portfolio now looks like this:

Fund	Amount
iShares Canadian Composite Index	$ 13,000
iShares S&P 500 Index	$ 12,000
iShares MSCI EAFE Index	$ 12,500
iShares Canadian Bond Index Fund	$ 13,500
Total Portfolio	**$51,000**

Let's assume that you have saved an additional $1,000 and you wish to add it to your portfolio this year. Since your portfolio is currently worth $51,000 (from the figures above), by adding $1,000, you will have a total of $52,000. Since your original goal is to have 25% of your money in all four funds, you would have:

$52,000 divided by 4 ETFs = $13,000 (invested in each ETF)

You will need $13,000 in each ETF to make it balanced (with the idea of maintaining 25% of your money invested in each fund). In this situation, by looking at the chart above, you would leave the Canadian Composite Index alone (as it's already at $13,000). You would buy $1,000 more of S&P 500 Index (US stocks) since it is only at $12,000 right now and you need $13,000 in each fund. You would buy $500 of MSCI EAFE Index (international stocks) and sell $500 of Canadian Bond Index to bring them both to a balance of $13,000. By making these changes you have met your original target allocation (of 25% of your money invested in each ETF) and can now leave this automated account to work for you for another year – all done in less time than it takes to order lunch at a fast food restaurant!

With this strategy you are buying more of your "losers" (the investments that have decreased in value) and selling (or not buying) more of your "winners" (the investments that have increased in value) – in essence you are "buying low" and "selling high".

An interesting little example from the magazine *"The Economist"* might help explain the power of this approach of buying low and selling high. The magazine created a fictional character named Henry Hindsight. In this example, he starts with only $1 and invests it in various markets around the world from 1900–2000 (I know it's a long time, but useful for explaining this idea). Every year he invests in the previous year's best performing investments (those investments that created the best returns the prior year). According to research, by following this strategy he ends up turning his initial $1 into $290. For an interesting comparison, if someone had simply invested $1 in the Dow (a list of the 30 largest stocks in the US) in 1900 and automatically reinvested the dividends, they would have ended up with $4,500 – much better then the approach of buying "last year's best performers" followed by Henry Hindsight. The mechanical nature of this rebalancing strategy forces you to do the opposite of Henry Hindsight.

Another advantage of this strategy is due to the fact you are investing in whole stock markets which constitute many stocks rather than a few individual stocks, your risk of a company such as Enron, Bre-X, or Nortel (companies that have gone bankrupt) derailing your portfolio is greatly reduced. You don't have to spend hours pouring over financial statements looking for the best companies. You don't have to be on the lookout for accounting "alarms" that warn you that the company you are thinking of investing in might be in trouble! You simply and mindlessly invest your money based on your original allocation once a year. With index funds your dividends (which are one of the most important factors in wealth creation) are automatically reinvested while ETFs will often pay you dividends which you can reinvest along with other money you are routinely adding to your portfolio.

Although this strategy may sound boring to some, you would in all likelihood outperform the majority of professionally managed mutual funds while spending less than 1 hour per year handling your portfolio. Remember the twin brothers investing example from the beginning of this chapter? A little extra performance can *double* your wealth in some cases – the difference can be huge! The next chapter will look at how you can reap even higher returns – if you are willing to give a little more effort (but not too much)!

8

DOING EVEN BETTER —
AND *STILL* BEING A
LAZY INVESTOR

*"You can't teach people to be lazy —
either they have it, or they don't."*
– Dagwood Bumstead

The last chapter looked at simple index funds and various ways you can create a portfolio in minutes that should perform very strongly over time. They key was avoiding the high fees often charged by mutual fund companies. The key here is if you can substantially reduce the fees you pay, you can keep more money in your own account and this money grows and compounds over time – enriching you instead of the financial industry.

Can you obtain even better investment returns? Can you avoid a substantial portion of the fees most average investors often pay and even get paid to invest in some companies? The answers to these questions are yes, yes, and yes – so let's take a closer look.

Here we will return to the subject of dividend reinvestment plans (DRIPs) – something that I covered in my second book, *"The Lazy Investor"*. The idea of these plans is that first, you buy the first share and order the share certificate. Second, enrol in the dividend reinvestment plan (DRIP) and share purchase plan (SPP). This strategy allows you to begin to accumulate shares over time – without paying any fees to the financial industry once you've acquired the share certificate. Getting the first share involves a process which I covered in great detail in my book, *"The Lazy Investor"* related to this strategy. Realize it does take a bit of effort to set these plans up initially. Once set up they require a minimum amount of time and effort to maintain (the whole process essentially runs on "autopilot"). My children who range in age from 2 years old to 9 years old, have portfolios set up with DRIPs and SPPs. The step–by–step process is all outlined in, *'The Lazy Investor: Start with $50 and No Investment Knowledge"*, however there is some additional information I would like to share with you.

The first issue involves deciding which stocks to buy. As I am a huge fan of dividend investing, the vast majority of my investment attention has focused on companies that pay out money (to me, the investor) on a regular basis in the form of dividends. When investing in stocks you should only consider stocks that pay dividends, but what is the actual process to know which stocks to pick?

I want to let you in on a little secret. In Canada, there are not a huge number of Canadian companies that have a long history of increasing their dividends on a regular basis. I've listed a lot of companies in my previous books, but here's a very simple way to construct your own portfolio of Canadian dividend–paying stocks.

The first step is finding a few Canadian dividend mutual funds (actual mutual funds that concentrate on investing in dividend–paying companies). The easiest way to do this is to go to *www.globefund.com*. You will notice at the top right corner of the site there is a box marked "search". In "search" box, type "dividend" and a list of many dividend mutual funds will appear. Choose a funds and click on it. Then scroll down and look at the top 10 companies the mutual fund is invested in. Write down the names on a piece of paper. Repeat this process (finding the top 10 companies) for a few other funds. By looking at a few different dividend mutual funds you

will have created a list of a number of good dividend–
paying companies (and a lot of companies will be a
top–10 holding in more than mutual fund). This process
allows you to see which companies the dividend mutual
funds have invested it.

Once you have a list of your potential companies,
you can go to *www.cdndrips.blogspot.com* to see the list of
companies that offer DRIPs. You can buy your first share
in any one of the companies you want to invest in that
also appear on this list. After you've completed this you
can enrol in the company DRIPs (dividend reinvestment
plans) and SPPs (share purchase plans). Another great
resource to learn more about DRIPs can be found at
www.dripinvesting.org.

The goals of this strategy are twofold – avoid all the
fees you regularly pay to the financial industry for
buying mutual funds, while *getting paid to invest in these
dividend-paying companies.*

> *If you are going to invest in shares, why not buy them in
> such a way that you get a discount? This can help you
> accumulate more wealth quickly!*

How can you attain this? First, find companies that
offer a discount to purchase their shares through the
DRIP. Once again, you can get this information by going

to *www.cdndrips.blogspot.com* and browsing the list seen on the site. Many companies offer a discount on the shares you purchase ranging from 1% to 5%. This gives you the opposite effect of paying mutual fund fees – which we looked at in the last chapter. Conversely, instead of paying a fee to buy shares through a mutual fund, **you get paid** to buy shares through a DRIP plan.

This information gives you an idea of how to earn more money by avoiding fees and getting stocks at a discount. But even though you are avoiding fees and buying shares at a discount, there are always risks with investing. The companies you invest in could go bankrupt or the general stock market could crash and reduce the price of the shares you own. What if you don't like the idea this sort of risk in your portfolio? What if you would like to benefit from owning some stocks or stockbased investments but you don't want to risk losing *any* of your money? That will be the focus of the next chapter.

9

INVEST IN STOCKS AND NEVER LOSE MONEY — *GUARANTEED!*

*"I would give all my fame for
a pot of ale and safety"*
– William Shakespeare

Investing in stocks and collecting dividends were a huge key for me reaching financial freedom at such an early age and countless other investors have had similar success with this approach. The key is doing it right – avoiding fees and sticking with companies that offer necessities people need and use daily (ie. water, heat, hydro, food, toothpaste) regardless of the ups and downs of the economy.

However, even using this approach, there are still potential risks if the companies you've chosen are poorly managed. If you are looking for an iron-clad method of investing so that you never lose your money while still benefiting from stock ownership, the following will guide you in a step by step approach which eliminates the risk of losing money.

Note that this strategy is best for RRSP accounts because of the way the investments are taxed. This strategy would not be as suitable for a portfolio held outside of an RRSP.

For example, suppose you currently have $100,000 in your RRSP. You decide you would like to invest in several stocks but also want to make absolute certain that you will not lose a single cent over the next ten years. Remember, stocks can have long periods of time where they lose money for investors (or shorter periods like 1929–1932 where investors lost almost 90% during this time). Here's how you can invest in stocks with a "safety-net" – a guarantee that even if the stock markets lose 90%, you would not lose a single cent – following these simple steps:

1. Buy an investment that will give you $100,000 in ten years – *guaranteed* (I will explain this investment below)

2. Invest the rest of your portfolio into stocks.

The first step in this process is to find a simple invest-ment that is guaranteed to give you your original $100,000 back in ten years. One possible investment that offers this peace of mind is an investment called "strip bonds" (or zero coupon bonds). I know you might be thinking "Here's he goes with the jargon", but this is all really simple.

First, to clarify, a bond is like a loan. When the Gov-ernment of Canada needs to raise money (aside from by taxing its citizens), it will borrow the money by selling bonds to people. For example, if you lend the Govern-ment $1,000 for 10 years and earn 5% per year, you would collect $50 per year for 10 years and at the end of 10 years the government would pay you your original $1,000 back. Here's how this scenario would look (on the chart below):

You lend the government $1,000 today. It pays you 5% interest per year, so you would collect the following interest payments:

Year	Interest Paid to You
1	$50
2	$50
3	$50
4	$50

5	$50
6	$50
7	$50
8	$50
9	$50
10	$50

Every year for 10 years you would collect a $50 interest payment. At the end of the 10 years, the Government would also give you your original $1,000 back. So you receive ($50 x 10 years = $500) in interest over 10 years and you also received your $1,000 back. This is as good a guarantee as you can get. Barring the Government of Canada going bankrupt or being overthrown by a hostile power, you *will* get your money back.

With a strip bond, it's a little different. Without getting into all the complexities, you essentially don't get the $ 50 interest payment every year, but instead receive all your money at the very end. So if you lend the Government $1,000 today, you would receive nothing for 10 years but at the end of 10 years you might get back $1,500 or some similar amount.

NOTE: This strategy I will show you would be for your
RRSP (or TSFA which we'll cover later) because of tax issues.

In order to accomplish this, you need to open up a self-directed RRSP at a discount brokerage. This can be done at any major bank and it should take around 30 minutes. If you have RRSPs outside a discount broker-age account, you can have them transferred to your brokerage account *without withdrawing the money.* The representative at the bank can help you do this and there should be no cost to do this. Make sure the brokerage company understands that you want the money trans-ferred to your self-directed RRSP account directly, because *if you withdraw the money yourself you will be taxed on it!*

So let's assume you've opened your brokerage account and transferred your money into it, so you have $100,000 in your self-directed RRSP discount brokerage account. Your first step is to buy a strip bond maturing in 10 years that will guarantee you a payment of $100,000. Remember, all you are doing is lending the Government an amount of money and they will pay you this amount back (plus interest) in one payment at the end of ten years. *Your dis-count broker should be able to walk you through the steps involved in doing this.*

At the time of this writing, you can buy strip bonds giving you $100,000 in a little less than ten years for only $69,162 (from the Government of Ontario). The remaining

$30,838 would be invested in the stock market. Here's how it would look:

Amount in RRSP to Invest:	$100,000
Less: Amount invested in Stripped Bonds	(69,162)
Amount Invested in Stock Market	$ 30,838

By utilizing the strip bond strategy, you have virtually guaranteed that you will have $100,000 in ten years. Let's take a look at a few possible scenarios for the stock market to see how this works in each case. We'll create two fictional characters – "Aggressive Al" and "Careful Carol". We'll assume Al puts all of his $100,000 into stocks whereas Carol uses this more conservative approach with her $100,000. Let's create 3 different scenarios:

1. **All the stocks the investors chose go to zero:**

   In the first situation, we're going to assume the absolute worst thing that could happen short of the disappearance of Canada itself. We'll imagine that *every single company* Al and Carol chose to invest in goes bankrupt. If they stick with the strategy of only investing in large companies with long histories that sell products or services people need, this scenario is probably as likely as the earth colliding with Mars next week. The list of companies they might have chosen would possibly include the banks, Bell Canada, Enbridge, Rogers Communications, and many other Canadian blue chip companies (blue chip companies are the biggest, safest kinds of solid companies). Could you see all of these companies going completely bankrupt? It's not very likely. Regardless, if this came to pass, here's how the situation would compare:

Al (who's totally invested in stocks) *loses all his money*. In other words, he's managed to turn his $100,000 into nothing. He's lost everything! This can and does happen with some very established companies – think Nortel.

In Carol's case, she suffers zero growth to her wealth over 10 years, but in the end she still has her $100,000. Therefore, she has not lost a single cent. This is because she has completely lost all the money she invested in stocks, but she's assured herself of keeping her $100,000 by buying the strip bond. She still has her full $100,000 even with all her stocks suffering total collapse!

Final Result (if all the stocks they chose end up in bankruptcy)

Al has lost all his money —
he has nothing: **Al = $0**

Carol still has her $100,000   **Carol = $100,000**

---

2. **Stock Investments earn NOTHING for 10 years:**
   In the second scenario, we'll look at what would
   happen if these companies continued to be viable
   ongoing businesses, but the stocks don't create any
   wealth for these investors for 10 years (even with dividends). I know we've all been conditioned to believe
   stocks always go up in the long-run, but the long
   run can be longer than most people have. Remember, US stocks did not increase at all in value from
   1964–1981 (or for 17 years). This sort of situation *can*
   happen again.

   In this situation, Al would still have $100,000 –
   he would not have gained anything over ten years.

   Carol would end up with the $100,000 guaranteed
   amount from her bond and an additional $30,838
   that she invested in stocks (since the stocks gained
   nothing over 10 years). So overall, she would end up
   with ($100,000 + $30,838=) $130,838 in total. She
   would have earned a little over $30,000 on her $100,000
   portfolio (around 30%) on her money (while keeping

her money totally safe) – and remember this is assuming a 10-year period where stocks gain *nothing.*

Final Result (If stocks gained NOTHING for 10 years):

Al has his original $100,000, but earned nothing	**Al = $100,000**
Carol now has $130,838 — gained over $30,000	**Carol = $130,838**

3. The Value of the stock investments double:

If Al and Carol's investment managed to double over the 10-year period, here's how it would look for our two investors.

Al would now have ($100,000 x 2=) $200,000 – a pretty reasonable return. He would have been pleased that he had chosen to invest his portfolio into stocks.

How about Carol then? Would she be upset that she chose to be totally safe? Carol would get her guaranteed $100,000 from her bond. She would also be happy to know that her stock investments would have doubled from $30,838 to $61,676. In total she would have $161,676 – so she would have earned over $61,000 on her money in 10 years.

Final Result: (If the value of stock investments doubled)

Al has grown his $100,000 into $200,000

Al = $200,000

Carol ha s grown her $100,000 into $161,676

Carol = $161,676

In this final scenario, Al ends up with almost $39,000 more than Carol. However, in order to realize this return, he had to take on more risk. Carol earned less, but perhaps slept more soundly during her 10 years of investing as she benefited from the peace of mind in knowing that she couldn't lose her initial investment.

Realize that the better the stock market does, the more money the investor who chose 100% stocks would do compared to the conservative investor. However, the investor who chose the guaranteed path would also participate in some of the gains of the stock market. The key here is that you are giving up some potential returns for the safety of virtually guaranteeing you don't lose money. Over the last few decades, buying stocks and keeping them for extended periods of time has been a great strategy. However, this has not always been the case throughout history and there's no reason to think it will continue to be the case forever. Having a built-in guarantee might not be a bad idea – even if you give up some potential return. You can alter the allocation depending on the amount of risk you're willing to take. For example, by placing half your portfolio in strip bonds and the other half in various stock index funds, you would still have pretty good portfolio protection with a better chance of gaining wealth with your stock index funds. Also the younger you are, the more stocks you probably want to own to keep up with inflation, so the amount you invest in bonds might be much smaller.

Once again, this strategy is most suitable for someone looking to invest inside their RRSP – or at least the strip bond portion.

The next chapter will look at how you can still collect dividend income but lower your risk of losing income due to dividend cuts (reductions). This strategy is more beneficial for people who are looking for income *outside of their RRSPs* – because of the tax benefits which I'll explain (in easy terms).

10

THE KIND OF SHARES YOU MIGHT "PREFER"

"October. This is one of the peculiarly dangerous months to speculate in stocks. The others are July, January, September, April, November, May, March, June, December, August, and February."
– Mark Twain

To date, all of my personal stock investments have been in what are known as "common" shares. Common shares are partial ownership in a company. The last chapter looked at investing in common stocks while ensuring you never lose money. In essence, you give up part of your potential return for reduced risk. With common shares, if you buy 100 shares of TD Bank let's say, you are a partial owner of the company. As such, your fortunes are somewhat tied to the company's fortunes. If the company earns more money, it might increase its dividends and you will then earn more income. If the company does poorly, the company might cut its dividend (reduce the amount of money you get paid).

The reason I've always liked common shares is because you are participating in the growth of the business and I needed growth in order to achieve my goal of financial freedom by my 30s. I try to minimize my risk by focusing on companies that offer essential products or services (ie. Gas, Water, Hydro). In addition to seeking companies that offer these necessities, I look for companies that have long operating histories and a strong habit of increasing dividends. Finally, I try to invest in very simple companies that I can understand. For example, TD Bank is a company most people can understand. As the population has increased and as TD has offered more services and raised their fees – common shareholders have benefited. Here's a quick snapshot of how dividends have done over the last 10 years (per share):

Year	Dividend/Share
2000	$0.92
2001	$1.09
2002	$1.12
2003	$1.16
2004	$1.36
2005	$1.58
2006	$1.78
2007	$2.11
2008	$2.36
2009	$2.44

Back in 2000, you could have bought shares in TD for around $35 per share. You see the dividend in that year was $0.92, so you would have earned about:

$0.92 divided by $35 = 2.6%

However, the dividend has risen and now amounts to $2.44. So if you had purchased shares in 2000, you would now be earning almost;

$2.44 divided by $35 = approx. 7% per year on your original investment.

You can see that by investing in TD in 2000, your income would have increased nicely – going up almost

3 times. But in difficult times, dividends can get cut. During the Great Depression, dividends on the US stock market dropped 55%. Once again, the reason I like dividend-based investing is that over time they have risen considerably. Dividends in the US stock market have increased 100-fold since the 1929 low. To illustrate this further, if your Grandparents had bought a collection of blue-chip stocks in 1929 and these stocks had provided $10,000 per year in dividend income in 1929, they would now be producing around $1 million dollars per year in income!

However, you might be concerned with seeing your income decline during turbulent times. If your dividends were cut in half, it might put a serious dent in your current lifestyle. You might not be able to stomach the prospect of losing half your income and hoping it recovers quickly – so what can you do? Many investors allocate a portion of their savings to fixed income investments such as bonds or GICs so they can collect regular interest payments. This can be an option for some investors, but what if interest rates are very low (which is the current situation we are facing as I write this)? Also, interest is the highest taxed form of income, whereas dividends attract much lower tax rates. Let's take a quick look at the difference between earning interest income and dividend income using a simple example:

Let's assume your regular income (from working or pensions) is currently $40,000 per year. You have a portfolio of $200,000 which you can invest to earn 5% in either interest paying bonds or dividends (I'm randomly using these numbers to make the math easy in order to make the comparison). So you would earn:

$200,000 x 5% = $10,000

At the income level in this example, interest income is taxed at 31% whereas dividend income attracts a rate of 7.5%. Take a quick look at the difference in how much you earn *after tax* investing in dividends versus interest income (Note: This example uses Ontario rates in 2009, but the basic idea holds true across the country):

	Interest Option	Dividend Option
Income ($200,000@5%)	$10,000	$10,000
Less: taxes payable	(–3,100)	(–750)
Income After Tax	$ 6,900	$ 9,250

Note: I took these figures from the Certified General Accountants (CGA) Personal Tax Planning Guide. This is a great resource that you can pick up FREE at most major libraries in Ontario around tax time.

The basic message is – dividends are a better form of income to receive – *outside of registered accounts* (registered accounts are RRSPs or TSFAs, which we will cover in a later chapter). However, in some cases, dividends can get reduced, which would lower your income. So this strategy I will show you is a way to reduce the risk of dividend cuts and get greater stability of income without giving up the tax benefits dividend income can provide. That is by focusing on a special kind of share called "preferred" shares.

Preferred shares parallel bonds some ways. They often offer a set rate of return just like bonds but some also offer varied rates of return based on certain factors such as the prime interest rate. Generally speaking, preferred shares don't offer the potential to benefit from the growth of the business. However, your payments are safer than those from common shareholders because all preferred shareholders must get paid before common shareholders can receive their dividends.

Generally, preferred shares have many different variations and cannot be summed up easily in one chapter of this book. It is a broad enough topic that the information about preferred shares could fill up an entire book on its own – but this is not the aim of this book.

The easiest way for novice investors to benefit from the income preferred shares generate would be to invest in an ETF (low-fee funds that buy many different stocks or bonds). You can simply buy a preferred share ETF and add it to your "15-minute portfolio" and readjust the amounts annually (as explained with the "15-minute portfolio" chapter). An example of this type of preferred share ETF would be the Claymore S&P/TSX Canadian Dividend ETF. You can buy this EFT through a discount broker (just as you would with the other ETFs).

At the time of this writing, this ETF sold for around $16.50 per share and offered a dividend of 7 cents per month (84 cents per year). This works out to an income of:

$0.84 divided by $16.50 = over 5%

The idea of buying an ETF is that it is a simple, low-cost way to invest. It is possible that the dividend of this ETF might be reduced if some of its higher yielding preferred shares are replaced with lower yielding shares – which is a potential concern expressed by James Hymas during a recent conversation. However, overall having a portion of your portfolio invested in a preferred share

ETF can offer you reasonable income while also enjoying tax benefits (outside of your RRSP).

If you are a sophisticated investor and interested in learning more about preferred shares, there are a couple of websites James has created that offer various articles and other information. For a listing of information on Canadian Preferred shares go to *www.prefinfo.com*. Aside from information about specific preferred shares, you can also click on various articles on the left–hand side to learn more. In addition, he also publishes a monthly newsletter at *www.prefletter.com*. Here you can subscribe for a fee and see preferred share recommendations. James Hymas is basically Canada's Preferred Share Guru and he frequently writes various articles related to preferred shares (often appearing in a financial mag–azine I write articles for as well) – *Canadian MoneySaver www.canadianmoneysaver.ca*.

Preferred shares are another tool available to you in your "stop working" toolbox. They can offer fairly safe income along with the tax benefits of getting dividend income. You can easily add a preferred share ETF to your "15–minute portfolio" to add diversification.

So far we've looked at various strategies for you to earn a good income without taking on undue risk. Now let's move on to the GICs or Bonds you might have in your portfolio and offer a strategy for you to *earn more money without adding more risk* using a little-known strategy that can be very powerful.

11

BANKING SECRETS
BECOME YOUR SECRETS —
"KEEP IT IN THE FAMILY"

*"Banks are an almost
irresistible attraction for that
element of our society which
seeks unearned money."*

J. Edgar Hoover

How can you earn more money inside your RRSP without increasing your risk? Here is a strategy that would suit investors who have a reasonable amount of money in their RRSP (at least $50,000) but have a distinct need to have the plan grow. Common low-risk investing generally involves choosing safe investments that pay regular

interest such as bonds, GICs (guaranteed investment cer-
tificates), and simple savings accounts. This chapter aims
to show you how you can do better without increasing
your level of risk.

First of all, you need to understand how these standard investments work. Suppose you go to your bank
and buy a GIC. In this case, you will lend money to the
bank at a fixed rate and lock your money in for a fixed
term. At the time of this writing, you can get a 5–year
GIC from the major banks for around 2% (but you might
be able to get a better rate if you negotiate). So if you
invested $100,000 @ 2% in a GIC, you would earn:

$100,000 X 2% = $2,000 per year (in interest)

Why does the bank pay you 2% to borrow your
money? Banks turn around and lend this money out –
often for mortgages. Right now, a 5–year mortgage at the
major banks costs around 4.5%. So using these real–life
numbers as I write this, if someone were to get a $100,000
mortgage, they would pay:

$100,000 X 4.5% = $4,500 per year

(in interest, approximately as the mortgage payments are
calculated on a reducing balance of principal owing)

By borrowing from you at 2% and lending at 4.5%, the bank would earn approximately $2,500 per year on this money. If you think about it, the bank ends up earning more money than you do by using your money.

Note – some people might currently be paying very low rates of interest with variable mortgages (where interest rates fluctuate), but they are taking on added risk if interest rates rise. Regardless, this example is for a 5–year fixed mortgage.

Right now, you might currently be invested in GICs at your bank and be earning a paltry 2% on your money while at the same time paying the bank 4.5% for their mortgage. In other words you are losing 2.5% per year (or $2,500 per year) if we assume the $100,000 from above.

If this is you, perhaps you can bypass the banks and lend the money directly to yourself. As mentioned earlier, this strategy is suitable if you have a reasonable amount of money in your RRSP. If you do, you can create a "non–arms length" mortgage from your RRSP to either yourself or another member of your family (as defined by blood, marriage or adoption). There are some processes to follow and fees to pay, but overall it can be a very powerful wealth–building tool. As this is not a common approach to mortgages, it is very possible your banker may not be familiar with the benefits of an RRSP mortgage, or the steps of the process. Given that, I recommend you ask your banker if they know how to process a non–arms length mortgage.

Here's a quick summary of what you have to do:

First, you must have a self-directed RRSP. If you do not, your bank (or more specifically their discount brokerage arm) can set one up free of charge. Then you will need to pay a set-up fee for the mortgage (usually around $100). Please note that there is also a $200 annual fee that must be paid. The recipient of the mortgage will have to pay CMHC (Canada Mortgage and Housing Corporation) a premium regardless of the amount of the downpayment. This is a requirement of Revenue Canada and it is to ensure that the mortgage will be paid back. If not for this requirement, an investor could theoretically withdraw funds from their RSP without having to pay tax on that income by not paying the mortgage back. As an example, if your mortgage amount was less than 65% of the value of your home, the CMHC premium would be 0.5%. The advantage here is that your mortgage is now CMHC insured, so it's safe! The only other fee involved is legal fees to set it up – perhaps a one-time $600–$800.

All these fees seem expensive, so let's look at the final result (using the interest rates from the example at the time of this writing). We'll assume you are lending $100,000 to an adult child. If the mortgage amount was greater than 75% of the value of the home, your child would pay the CMHC fees whether he or she borrows from the bank or from you – so there's no difference there. Let's compare "keeping it in the family" and making the RRSP mortgage versus buying GICs over 10 years. We'll assume setup costs of $100 plus $900 legal fees (to make it an even $1,000 for simple math) paid out of your pocket and ongoing $200 annual fees.

Since there are no legal fees to pay when you buy a GIC, we'll assume in the GIC example that you deposit the extra $1,000 (the fees you have to pay to set up the RRSP mortgage) into the GIC account (this is why it starts with $1,000 more). In addition, with the GIC option you also don't have the $200 annual fee, so we'll also add that to the GIC every year. Here's how your $100,000 would grow over 10 years if the interest rates remain as they are today:

Year	RRSP Mortgage (4.5%)	GICs (2%)	
Start	$100,000	$101,000	*($1,000 extra from fees)*
1	$104,50 0	$103,220	
2	$109,202	$105,484	

3	$114,116	$107,794
4	$119,251	$110,150
5	$124,617	$112,553
6	$130,225	$115,004
7	$136,085	$117,504
8	$142,209	$120,054
9	$148,608	$122,655
10	$155,295	$125,308

Difference ($155,295 – $125,308 = $29,987)

Note: Usually a mortgage must be amortized (paid off) over a period of time, but I've looked at interest-only calculations here to keep the comparisons similar to show you the effect of the extra interest has on your wealth.

By doing the RRSP mortgage, you have earned substantially more money – and this is after all the fees have been paid! In addition, the person who is paying the mortgage (either yourself or your adult child) has paid exactly the same amount as if they had taken out a mortgage from the bank. So basically you are "keeping it in the family" and not giving your money to the bank. It is also important to understand that as you make each regular mortgage payment, you are increasing the cash component of your RRSP as you decrease the amount owing on the mortgage. This money can be re-invested in the form of dollar cost averaging to ensure that it is not sitting idle. So for example, as mortgage payments are made to your RRSP, you can use these payments to gradually purchase index funds (as we saw earlier in the "15-minute portfolio").

The RRSP mortgage described above is called a "Non-Arms Length" mortgage because you are keeping the money within the family (what Revenue Canada calls non-arms length). Realize that you can also lend money to yourself (through what's called an "equity take-out) to purchase a second property (such as a cottage), or even for investments – which would make the interest tax-deductible. With these mortgages, you must charge the market rate of interest and the mortgages must be insured, usually through CMHC. There are other mortgages available called "Arms-Length" mortgages where you can lend money to non-related people. These mortgages are more flexible in the rates you can charge and they also don't need to be insured, *BUT I would advise against these for the less sophisticated investor.* These types of mortgages would be more risky, and not suitable for novice investors.

As mentioned, many bankers are not familiar with RRSP mortgages. If you encounter difficulties, call TD Waterhouse RSP Mortgage Department at 1-800-267-5759 (this is the bank I am familiar with).

The reality is that there are many opportunities using mortgages within your RRSP, but a whole book could be written on that topic alone. To keep things simple, I'll stop there. Just realize that by "becoming the bank" for either your own mortgage or your children's mortgage, you can increase the value of your RRSP without a huge increase in risk. Think about it. Have you ever heard of a bank making "record profits"? Why not get in on a little of that money to help pay for your retirement?

In keeping with the idea of earning more money without increasing your risk, the next chapter will look at the easiest way to do this – by paying less in tax. Let's take a look at the recently introduced TSFAs (Tax-Free Savings Accounts) and see how they work – and how they can help you.

12

TSFAS — NEW PLAN ON THE BLOCK...THAT CAN MAKE YOU WEALTHY

"The trick is to stop thinking of it as 'your' money."
– IRS auditor

In February 2008, the federal government unveiled a budget. The government had already cut taxes and reduced the GST, so the proverbial cupboards were bare. But with this backdrop, the government unveiled the best new plan Canadians have seen since the creation of RRSPs – the Tax-Free Savings Account (TSFA). Don't ask me why all the financial terms have to use a mix of letters that don't mean anything to the average person, but in keeping with the thinking of Shakespeare when he said, "A rose by any other name would smell as sweet.", these plans are the best thing that could happen to investors in a long time.

How do TSFAs work?

Just when most people were getting used to the workings of RRSPs (Registered Retirement Savings Plans) and RRIFs (Registered Retirement Income Funds), along came RESPs (Registered Education Savings Plans). I sometimes refer to these plans as the financial "3 R's", so at least you have to give the government credit for coming up with a plan that starts with a new letter!

TSFAs allow any Canadian taxpayer over the age of 18 to put aside up to $5,000 per year into this account. They are different than RRSPs in the sense that the person who contributes to these plans gets no tax–deduction. So basically – you earn money, you pay tax, then after that, anything left over can be invested into a TSFA.

What is the difference between investing in a "normal" non–RRSP account and a TSFA? The benefit of the TSFA is seen when and if you need to withdraw from the account. Any money withdrawn from TSFAs is *tax-free*! In fact, it's not even counted as part of your income in the year you take it out. This distinction might seem unimportant, but when you realize that many programs such as the Child Tax Credit or Old Age Security are clawed back based on your income, this benefit is important. Money earned and withdrawn from the TSFA does not affect your benefits (it does not trigger any claw backs – money taken back from you because your income is above a certain amount).

This is a very important distinction for some people. RRSPs had a weakness for lower income people in the sense that once it came time to withdraw the funds, the withdrawals were counted as income and affected the eligibility of some income support programs. In essence, they *discouraged* savings for lower income people, which is the exact opposite of what they were intended to do.

The other benefit of the TSFA is that you can take the money out anytime (tax-free as I mentioned), and then you may put that money back into your TSFA at a later date. Let me give you an example to explain:

Suppose you have $10,000 in your TSFA. Suddenly, you find out your roof needs to be repaired at a cost of $8,000. You don't have any money in your bank account, so you have basically two options – borrow the $8,000 or use your TSFA money. In the TSFA, you can withdraw $8,000 and pay for your new roof. Then you can save up the $8,000 over time and deposit it back into your TSFA where it will once again earn income tax-free.

So you can replenish the amount you withdrew any time in the future. For many people, these accounts are tailor-made for fulfilling one of the typical "cardinal rules" of financial planning – keeping an emergency fund in case you encounter a problem. An RRSP would not be a wise choice for fixing your roof because if you withdrew the $8,000, this amount would be taxable in the year you took it out. In addition to this, once you withdraw money from you RRSP, you can never replace it.

Who should open a TSFA?

A simple answer would be anyone who has money to invest should open a TSFA. Whether it's better to open an RRSP or a TSFA is a question that depends on your personal circumstances. One option for some people would be the "double down approach" – invest in a RRSP and then use the tax refund that it generates to add to your TSFA. Regardless, any other money that you have earmarked for regular investing outside of an RRSP should be invested in a TSFA. If you are married, your spouse should open one as well. If your spouse does not have the money, you can contribute to his/her TSFA without any tax implications. In other words, married couples can contribute $5,000 each ($10,000 total) per year into these accounts. The advantage of this is that when the money is taken out, any gains will be tax-free. You cannot open a TSFA for your minor children because you have to be 18 or over to have one of these accounts.

Once more I'd like to reiterate what I've said before. Paying off your mortgage offers a very good risk-free, tax-free return. So if you have a mortgage still outstanding, it might be better to focus on paying it off as quickly as possible before starting to invest. Once the mortgage has been eliminated, then you can divert the regular amount you usually pay on your mortgage into your RRSP and then use the tax refund it generates to contribute to your TSFA and "catch up" on all your unused room.

Another factor is if you are not able to contribute the $5,000 every year into your TSFA ($10,000 per couple), the amount you can contribute keeps going up. So let's suppose you are married but you currently have many expenses and you can't save anything into your TSFA for 5 years. Every year (as a couple), you are allowed to save ($5,000 each x 2 people = $10,000 per year). So if you can't save any money into the plan for 5 years, you would have ($10,000 x 5 years = $50,000) of available contribution room. Now suppose you suddenly find out that you are entitled to a $50,000 inheritance. In this case you could put the full amount into TSFA accounts and then all the income earned on the inheritance would be tax-free – *forever!*

If you are a young person starting out and saving up for a house – the TSFA is not the best option. For buying a house, you might want to max out your RRSPs to save for the down payment instead of using a TSFA. This is because you get the tax deduction which allows you to build wealth more quickly (you are saving with pre-tax dollars – the ones you get before the government gets its share). Again, one option might be to max out your RRSP and then use the tax refund you earn to contribute to your TSFA. Then when you buy your house (and everything costs more than you had planned), you can use the "Home Buyers' Plan" to take out the money from your RRSP (up to $20,000 tax-free) for the down payment, and then use the money you've built up in your TSFA to help make the repayments during the first few years.

*Note: Money taken out of RRSPs for the Home Buyers Plan is interest-free, but still must be paid back over 15 years to avoid being taxed on it. The money you added to your TSFA could be used to make the RRSP repayments for the first few years when finances might be tight.

I am just trying to give you some general ideas on how these plans can best be used to your advantage. I won't go into great detail here because a whole book could be written on these plans alone, but hopefully this information has given you some general ideas.

What should you invest in within your TSFA?

This is a difficult question to offer a "one size fits all" answer. First, if you are planning on using it (at least initially) to build up a safe, accessible emergency fund, you can simply open up a TSFA savings account. This would operate the exact same way as a regular savings account – except that the interest (what little you receive these days), would be tax-free. In addition, right now some financial firms offer slightly better interest rates because they want to attract new accounts. In addition, you should be able to get an account that is covered by the CDIC (Canada Deposit Insurance Corp) for up to $100,000 for an extra level of safety.

You might be content earning a small return with absolute safety, but what if you want to earn more? You can invest in stocks or bonds just like in regular investment accounts and enjoy the tax-free compounding.

Overall, these plans allow you to avoid tax on some of your investment income. They do not save you much initially, but over time the savings will become quite substantial. In addition, for those people eligible for some income support programs, these plans allow you to avoid the "claw backs". The basic point is that if you can increase your return without taking on additional risk, you should do it. These plans do that and if you have the money to invest, you should open one of these TSFA accounts.

This chapter is meant to give you a basic idea of how these plans work. If you are looking for a more detailed look, you might want to read more about them. One book I've found which offers some more information is," *Tax-Free Savings Accounts: A Guide to TSFAs and How They Can Make You Rich*" by Gordon Pape.

So that's the end of my low-risk investing ideas. The next brief chapter will outline how to piece all these ideas together depending on what stage in your financial freedom journey you are at.

13

---■---

"PIECING" IT
ALL TOGETHER

"He who fails to plan, plans to fail"
– Proverb

On the front cover of this book, you can see a "Stop Working ahead" sign. Exactly how far away you are from this goal can only be decided based no your current situation. This chapter outlines basic steps you can take to move you towards the goal – "Stop Working". The information in this book is designed for the novice investor and can set you on the road to reaching your goals. Once you have finished reading this book, you may feel more confident and comfortable investing for yourself. However, if you still feel you need assistance, you can consider obtaining advice from a "fee-only financial planner. For this service, you will pay a one-time fee (as opposed to the continuous percentage fees that can cost you over $1 million in some cases as we saw in Chapter 7 with the two fictional brothers. Whatever path you choose in order to reach your goal to stop working and enjoy a comfortable retirement, this can be your rough guide:

1. If You're just starting out:

If you are just getting started, the number one priority to follow is not to incur debt. Remember from Chapter 3 to also include car leases as debt and tackle it. Once you've paid off your car, start to save for your next vehicle while you're still driving the old one (so when you purchase your next vehicle, you will have a large down payment).

Once your other debts are paid, you should start saving for a home (if you don't already have one). One of the most efficient ways to do this would involve saving as much as possible in your RRSP (using low-risk investments such as short-term government bonds, money market funds, or simple RRSP savings accounts). If you are planning to use this money within a few years, the key is to focus on safety!

By contributing to an RRSP, you will receive a tax refund which you can deposit into your TSFA. Once you've found the home you like, you can take the money out of your RRSP without any tax penalties by using the "RRSP Home Buyers Plan" which you can Google to get more information. At this stage, if you are part of a defined contribution pension plan at your work, you probably want to contribute as much as possible to that plan if your employer matches your contributions.

At this stage you should be focused on:

- paying off all debt (and staying out of debt)
- saving as much as possible for a down-payment on your house (conservatively invested in short term bonds, money market funds, or other *guaranteed* savings)
- maximizing your defined contribution savings (that your employer matches)

2. If You're Already On Your Way:

If you are a little more established and already own your own home, it's time to move onto the fast track of planning. You should make certain you don't have consumer debt (and if so, eliminate it). Aggressively attack your mortgage using the tips I offered in Chapter 3.

At this stage you should be maximizing your contributions to your defined contribution plan (if you have one and your employer offers matching payments). If you started your career later on in life and work for an employer that offers a defined benefit plan, consider buying back a portion of your pension if you are entitled to. Ask your human resource department about this if it applies to you – some employers allow workers to do this.

While aggressively paying off your mortgage using the tips in Chapter 3, which should be a priority at this stage, any surplus money should be directed towards your RRSP and use the refunds for your TSFA. This money can be invested using the ideas from the "15-minute portfolio" in Chapter 7. This strategy will allow you to keep the fees to a minimum, but remember to rebalance your portfolio every year. If you don't want to risk what you've saved, buy some strip bonds (covered in Chapter 9) to protect all the money you already have, then invest the remainder into index funds or ETFs. If you have savings outside your RRSP or TSFA, consider starting DRIPs focusing on good quality stocks that offer discounts when purchased through a DRIP as we looked at in Chapter 8.

Once again, these are your savings goals, but you also want to use some money to have fun and enjoy life I'm not advocating a "slave and save" lifestyle, but do take care of your financial future using some of these ideas.

At this stage, you should be focused on:

- maximizing the benefits you will earn from employee pension plans
- eliminating your mortgage as soon as possible
- saving as much as possible in your RRSP (and using the tax refund to contribute to your TSFA)
- building up a financial portfolio outside of your RRSP and TSFA (if you can afford it)

3. If You're Almost There

If you are approaching the time to stop working, you need to get a basic idea of where you stand. This is where you should be looking at the pieces of your retirement "pie" (company pension, government pension, your home, and your personal savings). We covered this is Chapter 4.

At this stage you might realize that you already have enough future income to meet your lifestyle expectations after retirement. If this is you, relax and enjoy life! If not, ensure you are debt-free and pay off your mortgage as quickly as possible if you haven't already done so as we covered in Chapter 3. Keep contributing to your employee pension plans to maximize benefits.

With your personal financial portfolio, you might want to become more conservative by protecting what you've already saved using strip bonds by following the strategy in Chapter 9. Another option is that if you have a large amount of fixed income (bonds, GICs, etc) in your RRSP, you can look at getting a higher rate of return by creating a "family mortgage" covered in Chapter 11. If you still seem to be further away from reaching financial freedom than you had hoped at your age, take a look at the fictional couple "The Spendthrifts" in Chapter 5 and see if you can implement any of the ideas they used to reach their goals.

Another option is to continue working a few years longer and delay taking CPP so that when you do collect it, you will be entitled to a larger amount of money. Call 1-800-277-9914 for more information about this option.

Knowing your current financial situation is paramount but you may to closer to financial freedom than you realize.

At this stage, you should:

- calculate whether or not you already have enough income to retire in comfort
- if not – make sure you're completely out of debt (including your mortgage)
- look at the steps you might take to get you closer to retirement
- calculate how much more you need to save
- consider using a "family" mortgage (if this situation applies to you)
- consider using the "guaranteed" strategy using strip bonds to preserve what you have already saved
- Use the "15-minute portfolio" or DRIPs to continue building your wealth

NOW STOP...enjoy your retirement! You've earned it!

14

JOINING THE 21ST CENTURY... (BETTER LATE THAN NEVER)

"To err is human, but to really foul things up you need a computer."
– Paul Ehrlich

One thing I have discussed is that I am not someone who is into technology. I am typing this on my recently purchased laptop computer, which allows me to write almost anywhere – so it's been a great purchase. But I am sure I will be the last person in Canada without a cell phone as I still don't have one and have no plans of getting one. Overall, I am not very "tech-savvy", but I have received so many emails from readers asking me to add useful content to my website that I'm *finally* going to respond. Either in the fall of 2009 or early 2010, I plan on revamping my website at *www.stopworking.ca* with more content and perhaps a blog and/or an e-letter where you can often go to read articles or other information that might be helpful. I will try to address questions that readers pose through email and offer my thinking on things. I plan to make this website free of charge so that anyone can come by and benefit from a quicker exchange of information and perhaps I can provide updates to my strategies. This is new to me so feel free to send along any ideas you have at *www.stopworking.ca*.

One more quick note to readers:

I strongly feel that investing is not only about accumulating wealth. For me, it's about having enough money to enjoy life without being dependent on a job. This does not mean that I never want to work again – in fact I like working. *I just like doing it on my own terms!*

Some people have told me that the moniker I use on my books as *"Canada's Youngest Retiree"* is misleading, because they feel that I have not stopped working – because I've written some books. I guess it depends on your definition of "retirement" as in reality I never want to stop doing work whether it be volunteer work or pursuing my interests. Regardless, I understand the point some people have raised which is why I've changed my moniker on this book to "Canada's Millionaire Investor".

This term means that if I were to sell everything I owned I would have over $1 million without any debt. I spent a large portion of my 20s seeking adventure – whether it was backpacking around Europe, exploring Australia and New Zealand, moving to Vancouver, or working in Asia. During this time, I gradually built up a fairly large investment portfolio through regular investing and finally reached the "millionaire" milestone in my 30s without having won the lottery or inheriting wealth. The process mostly involved investing small amounts of money in good quality companies that pay dividends. I've also invested a portion of the income I've received from my books since I left the rat race and wrote *"STOP WORKING: Here's How You Can!"* almost six years ago. Realize there are many people much wealthier than I am but I can live a comfortable lifestyle with what I already have. The point is that my approach can be followed by anyone. Having the freedom to do what you want, when you want is a huge benefit. My investing approach has allowed me the freedom to pursue something that would be next to impossible to do without a regular income and a lot of free time – writing books. I hope some of the ideas in this book allow you to move closer to freedom – so that you can pursue your dreams. And remember, you may not need millions of dollars to **Stop Working Too!**

Appendix 1

---■---

FREE MONEY FROM YOUR RRSP!

*"The avoidance of taxes is the
only intellectual pursuit that
carries any reward."*
– John Maynard Keynes

This tip did not really fit into the idea of helping you retire as it is a quick manoeuvre that can earn you thousands of dollars in tax savings without much risk or effort on your part – but it is not a long-term strategy. In addition, it's a strategy that's a little more involved than what you have seen so far, so *it's more suitable for sophisticated investors*. As such, it didn't fit in the main section of the book. Regardless, if this strategy can be used to save you some money, you'll be glad you took the time to read about it here. You can check with your accountant for any subtleties, but here's the idea in a nutshell – so let's take a quick look:

1. The Quick Payoff

RRSPs can be very effective tools for planning for retirement. They are not an investment by themselves, but instead another account that is treated differently than regular accounts. The big advantage is that every dollar you contribute is tax-deductible, so if you are in a higher tax bracket while you are working, you can contribute money into your RRSP and get a large portion of the money you contributed back – through a tax refund. Once you retire, if your income is lower than while you were working, you will pay a smaller amount of tax on RRSP withdrawals.

Here's an example to help you understand this:

Suppose you earn a high salary and your highest marginal tax rate is 40%. In this case, if you withdraw $100 from your bank account and contribute that $100 to your RRSP, you would save $100 x 40% = $40 in tax. In other words, you could take $100 out of your bank account and deposit it into your RRSP and the government would give you $40 in tax savings to put back into your bank account (so in total it would cost you only $60 to invest $100 in your RRSP).

When it comes time to retire, your income might be lower, so you might now only be in the 25% tax bracket. Now when you take the $100 you invested out of your RRSP and put it back into your bank, you will only pay $100 x 25% = $25. So you saved $40 in taxes when you put the money into your RRSP and you only paid $25 in taxes when you took the money out – so overall you saved ($40 – $25=) $15. This is one of the key benefits of contributing to RRSPs. The other is tax-free compounding – but this factor does not really affect this particular strategy, so let's ignore that aspect for now.

Here would be a way for you to earn some instant money from the government if you are a high income earner about to retire with a lower pension income (or if your income will be lower or non-existent next year). If you are in a high tax bracket (again let's use 40% for simplicity), but have a lot of room in your RRSP to contribute (you can find that information on your "Notice of Assessment" from Canada Customs and Revenue Agency) and are about to retire (or will

have low income next year), here's an idea. Let's
explain using a simple example:

Suppose you have $30,000 that will be taxed at
40% this year, but since your income will be lower
next year, you will only be taxed at 25% next year.
You could deposit $30,000 into your RRSP in Decem-
ber of this year and withdraw it in the following year.
Look at the net effect of this:

This year, you save (in taxes): $30,000 x 40% = $12,000
Next year, you pay (in taxes): $30,000 x 25% =   (7,500)
Total Free Money $ 4,500

Note that when you withdraw your money from
your RRSP, there is a withholding tax. These withholding amounts look like this:

Withdrawal Amount	Withholding Rate (%)
Up to $5,000	10%
$5,001-$15,000	20%
Over $15,000	30%

These are withheld when you make your withdrawal and then when you do your taxes, you either
get some of the withheld amount refunded or you
have to pay the difference depending on how much
tax you owe.

To keep the withdrawal rates low, you could create accounts at a few different banks of just under $5,000 so that the amount withheld on your total $30,000 is just 10%. Otherwise you can simply take the full $30,000 out from one RRSP, pay the 30% withholding tax and then get the balance of your money back at tax time. Either way, the end result is that this simple manoeuvre can create a few thousand dollars with an hour's work.

If you don't have $30,000 lying around, you can look into getting an RRSP loan. Realize this would only be a short-term loan to get the tax benefit for contributing to your RRSP. You would probably have to make monthly payments until you've received the tax refund, so it would be best to take the loan out in early December. Each bank has certain offers, restrictions and fees so ask your bank for the details on their offers. This will require some research and legwork on your part, but the final rewards may be well worth the effort. Without commenting on the rules at different banks, here's a basic idea of what you can do.

Take out a $30,000 RRSP loan from the bank (usually at a low rate of interest) and put the $30,000 into your RRSP. This money should be invested in absolute safe investments – such as an RRSP savings account. After the New Year arrives, withdraw all the money from your RRSP (less the amount for withholding taxes) and pay off a large chunk of the loan (RRSP loans can usually be paid off at any time, but make sure with your bank beforehand). You would then pay off the remainder when you get your tax refund. Remember you are getting this refund because you made the RRSP contribution.

Here's the net affect on you (ignoring small fees which you will probably pay) if you deposit the money into the RRSP, then withdraw it to pay back a portion of your RRSP loan:

Get RRSP loan (December)	$30,000
Withdraw RRSP (less 30%	
withholding — in the New Year)	-(21,000)
Balance Owing on RRSP loan	$ 9,000

You have to keep the loan for a few months until you get your tax refund based on your RRSP contribution. From our example, you would get:

($30,000 RRSP Contribution x 40% tax rate) = $12,000 tax savings

You would take $9,000 (plus nominal interest and fees) from your tax refund and pay off the remaining balance owed on the RRSP loan. The remaining (almost) $3,000 would be yours to spend as you please – which you earned by spending perhaps an hour or two of time to set it all up at your bank.

Then, the following tax year you would receive another $1,500 free. This is because from this example you are now in the 25% tax bracket BUT you paid a 30% withholding tax, so the government would owe you the 5% difference on the $30,000 which works out to a free $1,500. In total you have earned almost ($3,000 + $1,500) = $4,500 for your efforts.

The other option is to use your home equity line of credit (if you have one). The point is that borrowing $30,000 for a short period of time will cost you very little, but the savings could amount to a few thousand dollars – with minimal effort or risk on your part.

If the ins and outs of this strategy seem a little too complicated for you – I understand. You might want to talk briefly with an accountant or fee-only financial planner to see if this strategy can help you. If it costs you a few hundred dollars for a professional to walk you through it, and you gain a few thousand dollars – it will have been well worth it.

Appendix 2

PORTFOLIO UPDATE

"I measure what's going on,
and I adapt to it.
– Martin Zweig

In all my books I have provided readers with an update of what I have been doing with my personal financial portfolio. This appendix follows that tradition and will give you a quick snapshot of my thinking. Let's start by taking a look at the stock market.

A Little Stock Market History...

Remembering that NOBODY KNOWS THE FUTURE, it is basically impossible to predict what you should do shorter term when pivotal events occur. However, as Mark Twain said," History doesn't repeat itself, but it does rhyme" – by looking at the factors we face right now, we can make a reasonable assumption about the *most likely* outcomes.

Think about it...most investors are familiar with the caveat, *"Past results are no guarantee of future returns"*, but can't past results at least guide us sometimes? For example, do you have a restaurant you like to go to? Chances are you keep going there because in the past you received good food and good service. Past results do offer a general idea of what you might expect.

Using history as a rough guide, let's examine the stock market. Let's choose 1967 as our starting point – the year the world-famous Big Mac was introduced.

When the Big Mac was introduced in 1967, it cost 45 cents while the average is around $3.57 today (in US dollars as the data is easier to find). In other words, the cost has gone up almost 8-fold over the last 40-plus years. During the same time period, housing has increased from $25,000 to $225,000 (about a 9-fold increase), new cars have gone up 10-fold, postage stamps 8-fold, gas 9-fold, ... There are many products that are much cheaper (such as electronics), but other items such as services are much more expensive (i.e.. health care and tuition fees). Regardless, the overall trend has created around an 8 or 9-fold increase in cost of living over the last 40–plus years. In other words, you would need approximately $8 or $9 today to buy what $1 would have bought you in 1967.

In 1967, the Dow Jones Average (general proxy for the US stock market) was trading at around 1000 points. It is currently around 9,000 – so overall it's had about a 9-fold increase since the mid-sixties. I am using US statistics here because they are more readily available, but generally Canadian stock markets will follow the performance of US stock markets to a large degree over the long term.

Think about it...If you had invested enough money in the stock market to buy 100 Big Macs in 1967, you would still have only enough money to buy around 100 Big Macs today (excluding dividends). This fact highlights the importance of dividends. The majority of the wealth that stock investing has created for investors have come from dividends. Dividends were a key component of my investment strategy and are *the reason* to buy stocks in the first place.

A closer look...

US Stock markets gained *nothing* from 1964–1981. An investor who had put money into stocks in 1964 would have had roughly the same number of dollars in 1981. BUT, inflation was very high during this time, so most investors lost wealth! The stock market was a *wealth-destroyer*, not a *wealth-creator* during this time.

Then from 1981–1999, stock prices rose 10–fold! During this time, an investment of $1 in stocks returned $10 to investors (excluding dividends). Becoming rich was as simple as putting money in the market and watching it grow – as simple as planting seeds and watching the flowers bloom! Since 2000, stock prices have not increased overall so investors have not earned a lot of wealth during this period – although some sectors have done better such as oil and gas.

The Next 2 decades...My Best GUESS

What does the future hold for today's investors? The reality is that NOBODY REALLY KNOWS. I am not in the stock market forecasting business as I am possibly the worst stock market forecaster in the world. My approach to retirement was created so that I could retire *regardless of what happens to stock prices*. I focused on buying companies with solid histories of increasing earnings and dividends. However, although we can't predict what will happen in the future, let's look at some factors which might affect things:

1. Interest rates
2. Boomers are getting older
3. People are up to their eyeballs in debt

Let's take a look at these factors...

1. Interest rates at historical lows

The main reason stocks performed so badly from 1964–1981 is because interest rates were rising. Interest rates were very low in the early 1960s but moved relentlessly higher into the early 1980s (anyone looking for a mortgage at that time might remember paying around 20% for a mortgage). When interest rates rise, stock prices go down. Here's why:

Assume you have $1,000 to invest and Canada Savings Bonds pay 10% interest. In this scenario you can simply buy bonds and earn a decent rate of interest. Your idiot brother-in-law can walk into any bank and buy bonds and earn a similar rate of return that stocks have earned over the history of the markets (approximately 10%). Many investors in this situation would buy bonds (and not stocks) because bonds offer a *guaranteed* 10%, whereas stocks involve much more volatility and risk. Therefore, since there are fewer buyers for stocks, the prices for stocks fall. This is what happened from 1964–1981.

Since 1981, the opposite has occurred with interest rates falling (and stock prices soaring)! Interest rates have fallen from 20% in the early 1980s to close to zero percent today – but they cannot fall any lower. That huge boost to stock prices has run its course.

2. Boomers are getting older.

Baby Boomers (those born from 1947–1966) are the most influential population cohort in North America. They are approaching the age where they will spend less and save more (older people generally follow this consumer behaviour). As consumers spend less, companies sell fewer products, so their profits go down – which causes their share prices to fall. In addition, as boomers get older, they will become more conservative in their investments. This means they will take money out of the stock market and invest it in safer options, which will be a negative factor for stock prices.

After the baby boom we encountered a "baby bust", where women had significantly fewer babies. Having a huge baby boom followed by a baby bust is unprecedented in history in North America. The only example of a similar situation occurred in Japan.

The baby boom in Japan ended in the early 1950s (around 15 years before the baby boom ended in North America). Japanese stock prices peaked in 1989 and have since fallen over 75%. This does not mean North American stock prices will follow the exact same path, but an aging population is a drag on stock prices.

3. People are carrying a lot of debt

Over the last few decades people have taken on incredible amounts of debt and this debt will have to get repaid eventually. As debt is being incurred, people are able to live beyond their means, so they spend more money which boosts company profits – and hence stock prices. This debt accumulation has been a boost, but once debt starts getting repaid, it will be another drag the stock market.

With these three realities it's quite possible stocks won't perform like they have since the early 1980s.

Unforeseen events may happen which will keep the stock prices rising for a long time to come – but there are risks. History shows that there have been very long stretches of time when stocks were not great investments. All this is not to say that I think stocks are now a bad investment – you just have to keep realistic expectations and invest properly – focusing on dividends.

Dividends are what brought me my success and gave me early financial freedom. However, with the recent financial turmoil, some companies have cut (or eliminated) their dividend, so is this still a good strategy?

Is the Sky Falling...and What About Dividend Investing Now?

Is it time to get out of stocks forever? Is the dividend-based investing strategy dead? The short answer is no. Let's see how this strategy has worked for me using my portfolio I listed in my most recent book, *"Money for Nothing"* showing the original dividends I received in 2004, the dividends in early 2009, and the percentage change.

Holding	Original Dividend	Current Dividend	% Change
Algonquin Power	$0.92	$0.24	–(74%)
Canadian Oil Sands	$0.40	$0.60	50%
Corby Distilleries	$0.50	$0.56	12%
Enbridge Income Fund	$0.85	$1.15	24%
Encana	$0.20(US)	$1.60(US)	700%
Johnson and Johnson	$0.93(US)	$1.80(US)	109%
Livingston Int.	$1.15	$0.50	–(56%)
Manulife	$0.42	$1.04	94%
Pembina	$1.05	$1.56	49%
Pengrowth	$2.52	$1.20	–(48%)
Riocan REIT	$1.20	$1.38	15%
*Epcor	$2.52	$2.52	*no change*
George Weston	$1.44	$1.44	*no change*

*Note: My investment in Epcor was originally an investment in TransCanada Power before it was bought out

*Note also that the figures above for Canadian Oil Sands, Corby, and Encana are adjusted to account for their respective 5-for-1, 4-for-1, and 2-for-1 stock splits.

*Note also that after I had sold the two following holdings, Manulife cut its dividend by 50% — to $0.52 per share and Livingston eliminated theirs.

Overall dividend income increased and the strategy has worked as it was meant to since I stopped working. There had been some pretty serious dividend cuts (mostly during the 2008 financial tsunami), but the dividend increases over time offset these declines.

This investing approach has served investors well in the past – and it should also be good in the future – over the longer term. But you must be aware that dividend cuts can happen. Let's look at an example where I invested like an idiot and where that idiocy cost me as one of my holdings suffered a massive dividend cut.

Bank of America, as the biggest bank in the world's largest economy with over 30 years of consecutive dividend increases seemed like a great investment. In fact, they had avoided a lot of the troubled sub-prime mortgages (risky mortgages) that had become so common in the US in 2007 and 2008. Regardless, this bank made a couple of untimely acquisitions and suffered huge losses. They responded by cutting their dividend from 64 cents to 1 cent (not a typo). This was an early warning of the potential rot within the financial system.

There were many other firms cutting their dividends at this time. When the entire system is tainted with backroom deals and hidden problems all over the place – I get worried. In the US, the whole banking system was on the verge of collapse and only survived with the aid of billions of dollars from the US government. Other companies required bailouts to keep from closing their doors. With potential problems being exposed in 2008 and other potential problems being unknowable in advance, I took a defensive stance and **sold my shares**. I took this extreme action for two reasons:

1. Not knowing hidden problems:

In some ways, investing is like searching for a place to live. If you walk into a home, turn on the lights and see a cockroach – you can be sure there are more – there is never just "one cockroach". Similarly if you find out there are some problems, chances are there are more lurking somewhere underneath the surface. For example, Nortel kept reporting accounting problems for years until its eventual demise. When there are major problems surfacing daily and you can't measure the extent of the potential problems – you take action.

Once US financial stocks began cutting dividends, I became concerned that it could happen here in Canada. Our financial companies have been more conservatively managed, but there was still the potential for trouble. Although I've made my share of idiotic mistakes, selling my shares proved wise when Manulife cut it's dividend by 50% a few months after I sold it.

2. I could actually earn more income (with less risk) by NOT owning shares

When there is turmoil in the stock markets, the financial media often makes bold and ridiculous claims. One example is an article from a major US financial publication which ran a headline, *"What's Wrong, Warren?"* with a picture of Warren Buffet and the caption, *"Warren Buffett's taste for technology has soured performance."* The idea of the article was that Warren Buffett had avoided high technology stocks and that had been a huge mistake!

Over the next few years many technology companies went bankrupt and investors lost a lot of money. Avoiding investments in technology companies ended up being a wise move.

Another famous article appeared in a highly respected financial magazine entitled, *The Death of Equities"* (equities mean stocks). Written in 1979, the article explains why stocks were going to be a terrible investment for a long time. The very next year, the stock market started on its multi-decade journey of incredible gains for those people who had invested in stocks.

In both cases the financial media was dead-wrong.

When I explained that I had sold my stocks, the response was massive overreaction. Internet chat rooms lit up with talk about the "dividend strategy being dead" or the strategy of dividend investing being a flop. Others argued that my original Stop Working strategy was no longer valid. This sort of hysterical overreaction is common when stock markets crash – but history has shown these knee-jerk emotions to be inaccurate longer-term. To get a more reasoned, less emotional view of how the dividend-based strategy might fair, let's look at how it performed during a very difficult period – the Great Depression.

Dividends in the US fell by around 55% from 1929–1931. However, it's important to note that during this period there was severe deflation (falling prices) of around 25%. This means that after deflation, you only needed $75 to buy what would have cost you $100 before deflation. So in keeping with our "Big Mac" example, if you initially earned enough money from dividends to buy 100 "Big Macs" before the dividend cuts, you had enough to buy:

45% (new income amount) divided by 75% (new
prices) = approx 60

So the number of Big Macs you could buy
dropped from 100 to 60 – not great, but not the end
of world scenario either. Even though "Big Macs" were
not invented until much later, the example is useful
for a simple illustration of what happened.

Then between 1931 and 1936, dividends more
than doubled! In other words, dividend investors
suffered a setback to their income in 1929 that was
pretty much fully restored by 1936. It is also important to note that **dividends have risen 100-fold since
the low of 1929!**

Dividend investing is NOT dead and continues
to be one of the best ways to invest in stocks. There
will be dividend cuts from time–to–time, but overall
dividends rise and this puts more money in your
pocket. My children are all still DRIPping following
the strategy in, *"The Lazy Investor"*. This market turbu-
lence will help them build more wealth over time as
they gradually buy stocks at cheaper prices.

But isn't this a contradiction for me to say that I
think the dividend–based investing strategy is still
valid (history strongly supports this claim), and yet

I sold my dividend-paying stocks! Why would I do this?

The reason is that I can earn **higher returns with lower risk** by using the strategy I explained in my previous book, *"Money for Nothing and Your Stocks for FREE"*. However, it's important to realize that this strategy is complex and only suitable for sophisticated investors.

Let me give you a real-life example to explain this approach using a large Canadian stock – Manulife Financial. This company is one of the largest insurance companies in North America with a strong and growing presence in Asia. I have been a shareholder of this company for a number of years – and it has provided me with solid and increasing dividends over that time. However, when the financial crisis hit, I sold this stock at a price in the low 20s as I felt it was too risky with all the uncertainty in the financial system. The stock price plummeted to around $9 within a month of me selling it but has since recovered to around $21 at the time of this writing. The company also cut its dividend by 50% since I sold it. Whether this particular stock is a good investment or not is open to debate, but for our purposes let's assume that this stock is a good potential investment you might be considering.

If you bought this stock right now, you would pay $21 per share and collect a dividend of $0.52 per year. This means you would earn around:

$0.52 divided by $21 = around 2.5% per year

In this situation, you would earn 2.5% in dividend income per year.

With my strategy, I **offered to buy** the stock by January 2010 (it is September 2009 as I write this) for $20. This means that if the stock price falls to $20 or below, I am obligated to buy the shares for $20. For this promise, I earned $1.37 per share immediately. If I am forced to buy the stock for $20, my actual price will be:

$20 (stock price) — $1.37 (money received) = $18.63

If I don't buy the stock, this means I am earning:

$1.37 divided by $18.63 (amount "invested") = around 7.4% (in four months)

I am earning 7.4% in four months (or 22% annualized) using the strategy from my *"Money for Nothing"* book versus 2.5% (annually) by buying the stock – **so I am earning a much higher return**.

Generally, higher returns mean taking on greater risks – but not in this case. If I bought this stock outright, I would be paying $21 per share which I could lose if Manulife filed for bankruptcy. This means my:

MAXIMUM risk is $21 *if I buy the shares*

On the other hand, by offering to buy the shares for $20, I will immediately pocket a premium of $1.37 as shown above. Therefore my:

MAXIMUM risk is $18.63 *if I offer to buy the shares*

The maximum risks assume bankruptcy which is extremely unlikely, but the risk is less using the"*Money for Nothing*" strategy than if I buy the stock. If a more likely thing happens and Manulife shares decline by around 10% to $19 per share by January 2010, I would lose money by buying the shares but I would still earn a small profit using my strategy. **This risk of losing money is higher if you buy the shares.**

Your next question should be "What's the catch?" How can this strategy offer **lower risk and higher returns**?

If stock prices rise substantially, then I would "miss out" on those gains. However, I am willing to give up some potential capital gains for lower risk and higher income.

The reality is that we live in an imperfect and unpredictable world. If we could invest with the benefit of hindsight, investing would be easy – but that is not the way the real world works. With investing – as with many other things in life, you go with the odds. For example, insurance companies will charge a new 16–year–old driver higher rates than a 50–year–old. That doesn't mean that after the company underwrites the insurance that it's not possible the young driver never has an accident and the older driver quickly has two accidents – but the insurance company must look at the *most likely* outcome based on history and statistics.

It is my thinking that the stock markets will not increase as quickly over the next few decades as they have over the last few decades. Time could prove me dead-wrong on that assumption, but it is my best estimate based on the factors I believe are important. As such, I am willing to give up some potential "gains" for the benefit of lower risk and increased income.

The reason I included this appendix is not to encourage investors to follow my strategy – as it is not suitable for all but the most knowledgeable investors who have the time to research it. The reason I decided to include it is because there has been a lot of misinformation about my approach.

Dividend investing is **NOT** dead and I fully expect to reassemble a portfolio of solid dividend-paying stocks – gradually – at cheaper prices with higher dividends. In the meantime, I would prefer to earn higher income while taking lower risks.

Warren Buffett, surprised many people when he sold all his stocks in the partnership he managed in the late 1960s and returned all the cash to his partners because he felt the stock market didn't offer good value. However, he is still held up to be the quintessential "buy and hold" investor – but he adapted to circumstances.

I've done the same thing for the time-being – adapted to circumstances.

If you have any questions or thoughts, please feel free to contact me through *www.stopworking.ca*. I am planning to offer more information on this site either late 2009, or in 2010 which will be free to all my readers. In the meantime I hope you've discovered some knowledge that will help you...**STOP WORKING TOO!**

FREE
INFORMATION
FOR **YOU**

I am planning on starting a blog or e-letter soon after this book is published. This will be a free service for my readers. I will post various articles from time-to-time (at my convenience since I don't want to work too hard). You can go to my website to read these archived articles as they appear. In addition, I might create an "e-letter" service where current articles will be sent to your e-mail (free of charge) as I write them. I'm not sure of the technical process as this book goes to print, but when we develop this, you will be able to subscribe for free at:

www.stopworking.ca

I hope to have this available for you soon...

Cheers,
Derek Foster